Raising the Perfect Family

And Other Tall Tales

By
GAYLE CARLINE

Cover art by Joe Felipe of Market Me
(**www.marketme.us**).

Published in USA by Dancing Corgi Press

DEDICATION

To my readers in Placentia—you mean the world to me!

ACKNOWLEDGMENTS

Thank you to Heather McRae and the Placentia News-Times for publishing my weekly musings.

Thank you to my husband Dale and our son Marcus for letting me talk about them in my weekly musings.

And most of all, thank you to the citizens of Placentia who read my musings and tell me how much they love them—or even how much they hate them.

I love you all.

CONTENTS

JUST KIDDING

Seriously, show me a perfect family. I dare you. As a matter of fact, I'll skip right ahead and triple-dog-dare you.

I was 38 years old when I married and had my son. By that time, I had convinced myself it wasn't going to happen. And then it all came rushing at me—soon I was juggling a husband, a son, a home, etc. You know… life.

In 2005, I began writing a weekly humor column for the Placentia News-Times, a local paper that is affiliated with the Orange County Register. My aim was to tell slice-of-life, Erma Bombeck-style stories of my life in the big little city of Placentia. Stories of "my" life naturally included my husband, my son, my home, etc…

Many people tell me how much they enjoy reading my tales, from appliance disasters to childrearing faux pas, and that many times, they've been through the same thing. I've enjoyed getting advice about where to get things repaired, and where to take Sonny Boy for sports, doctors, and driving lessons.

I thought I wanted to entertain my readers, but it turns out, I was looking for my community. I found more than that. I found friends.

I've been writing these stories for ten years now, and I plan to keep writing them until they kick me out the door.

But don't expect me to write about a perfect family. Not even if you triple-dog-dare me.

A CLEAN HOUSE—WHAT'S THAT?

I'd like to have a clean house all the time. When I lived alone, this was possible. I spent Saturday mornings cleaning my condo. I was rewarded with a glorious feeling of accomplishment as I sat on my vacuumed sofa with my cup of victory tea.

When I married Dale, however, I traded my clutter-free life for love. When Marcus was born, I traded cleanliness for the joy of motherhood. I also traded in my waistline, but that's another story.

Over the years, my housecleaning has adapted to my lifestyle. Between Marcus' school activities and our family outings, I can no longer schedule a day to clean the bathrooms and do the floors. When I first noticed this, I admitted defeat and stopped trying to clean. It was depressing to clean a room ten minutes at a time, spread over the week. How would I ever be done? Would I ever be able to enjoy a clean house again?

Before long, I had to do something, or risk losing my son in the mounds of pet hair. So I scaled back my expectations and began a system I like to call "clean what's bugging me most at the moment." Depending upon what I can't stand to look at, I mop a floor here, wipe a counter there, or dust a table somewhere else. The house never looks quite clean to me, but I figure I'm at least holding chaos at bay.

The one exception to this rule is when I am entertaining. That's when the old me resurfaces to scrub baseboards and dust behind furniture. I spend at least two full days, straightening and cleaning every room in our house—with the exception of Marcus' room. I haven't found a bulldozer that will fit through his door yet.

Dale and Marcus have amusing responses to my efforts. My husband looks worried; he knows this is how I'd like to have things all the time, and I think it makes him uncomfortable. It seems to raise the bar for a man's behavior, as if they have to now be careful of setting a glass on a table, or messing up the pillows on the sofa. Dale may think he has to put on a tie to watch the Laker game when the house is this clean.

Marcus is usually thrilled by the cleanup.

"Wow, this looks great, Mom," he tells me. "We should keep it like this all the time."

Then he throws his backpack in the middle of the family room and kicks his shoes off in the doorway. He is very surprised when I yell at him to take his stuff to his room. (I think I just heard a collective "Duh" from every mother on the planet.)

I recently had to host a meeting of our VHS Choir Dinner Theater Committee. We had decided, at the very last minute, that my house was the only available home for a get-together. It was a very panicky morning for me, as I raced around, cleaning every visible surface in the dining room, living room, family room, kitchen, and guest bath. I used the bedrooms to store all of the clutter and shut the doors.

When I closed Marcus' door, I noticed dark droplets at the bottom, as though something had splashed there. That's when I realized the shadow on the carpet was actually a stain. I confronted him with the evidence when he got home.

"Yea, I see it," he said. "But I don't know how it got there."

At that moment, I'd have taken a little less motherhood joy for a little more cleanliness.

THE RELUCTANT STUDENT DRIVER

Prepare to slow down, everyone. My son got his learner's permit.

I know, the usual joke is, "Stay off the road! My kid's learning to drive!" Parents tease that they're unleashing speed demons, even though I know they're expecting better behavior than that from their children. In my case, I fear just the opposite, that I'm turning an uber-cautious driver loose on the streets.

It took me almost six months to convince Marcus to take a driver's education course. He wasn't confident in his ability to make good decisions and was afraid of getting into an accident. I explained that if he studied the rules of the road and spent enough hours behind the wheel, he would be as good a driver as anybody else.

Then I signed him up for an online course. It took another six months for him to complete it, and only after I threatened to sign him up for a second course that would make him sit in a classroom on Saturdays. At last, he was ready to start learning how to drive.

If only it was that easy. The entire driver's licensing system seems designed as a model of "which came first, the chicken or the egg?" First, you complete a written course and get a certificate. Then you sign up at a school to get your behind-the-wheel training, except that they can't officially enroll you until you have your learner's permit, which you can't get until you've signed up at the school...

Basically, we went to the school with one certificate in order to get another certificate to take to the DMV, to get the provisional learner's permit to take back to the school. Got that?

I made an appointment for the Fullerton DMV office at 4 p.m. on Monday. Although I tried to get Marcus there ahead of time, traffic was unreasonable and we screamed into a parking space with two minutes to spare.

The office was everything I expected and more. Marcus' appointment confirmation instructed him to go to the "Start Here" line; which extended out the door. On a whim, I went inside and looked around. Stapled to a column was a small sign in faded ink: "Appointments start at Window #20."

They really want you to pay attention at the DMV.

Marcus got into that line, and got a number, just in time for their computers to crash. I wondered if they'd send us home, but a really nice woman with a really big voice took charge. Good thing she worked there. She looked at Marcus' number, then spotted a co-worker who wasn't busy.

"Here," she told the guy. "You've got a customer."

He processed Marcus' paperwork, took my money, then told Marcus to go to Camera 1 for his picture before heading to take the written test. Marcus entered the blue door to the testing room at ten minutes before five, and I began to think we'd get out of there before closing time.

By twenty after five, I wondered where my son was. People who had gone in after him were already coming out. Finally, he appeared, a wide smile spread across his face. He was leaping for joy as we went back to the car.

"What took you so long?" I asked.

"I didn't want to rush," he told me. "I only got two wrong!"

"Pretty happy to have your learner's permit?" I asked.

"I'm just happy this part is over," he said.

So, be prepared to follow the car traveling one mph under the speed limit. Try not to tailgate; he is my son.

DEATH OF AN APPLIANCE

With one horrid pop and a few choice words, my family was thrust into the Dark Ages this weekend. The microwave broke. I was not actually present during the event. As a matter of fact, I had just heated a little pasta for my lunch, with no problem. Later, on my way back into the kitchen, Dale gave me the bad news. The microwave was not heating, instead it was making a noise that sounded like the whole thing would explode any second.

My approach to problem solving is a little different than Dale's. When the plumbing leaks, I want to call the plumber, immediately, no matter what time it is. Recently, my washing machine began to growl like a Wookie and stopped letting water into the tank. My gut reaction was to go to Sears and get a new one. It was Sunday night at eight, but I didn't care; I'd wait by their door until the next morning.

Dale, on the other hand, wants to make certain the broken object can't be repaired. He is the original eco-friendly guy. He will dismantle the pipes or machine to see if he can figure out what the problem is. He'll even read the manual and search around on the Internet to find the right part. I'm in awe of his willingness to tackle projects, especially the ones where he has no experience.

Of course, I'd also like to wash clothes, or use the sink, or whatever, eventually.

The other piece of this equation is Dale's availability. He does work for a living, as an engineer. Engineers are salaried employees, working on projects with deadlines. This means that there is no "standard 40 hours" when a milestone needs to be met, and milestones are everywhere.

This also means that home repairs cannot be done in my time frame, which is within 30 minutes of breakage.

So when our microwave died, I took a deep breath and asked Dale what we were going to do about the problem. I should mention, at this point, that our microwave is mounted above our oven, which adds to the degree of difficulty in the fix-or-replace quandary.

"I think it's just a bulb that needs to be replaced," he said.

After two days without instant heat-ability, I asked if I should be doing something about the broken appliance, or if he would take care of it. He said he'd try to fix it.

Part of me is hoping he can just replace a piece and make the microwave work again. Finding another microwave that fits into the space above the stove is time-consuming and worrying—what if I buy it, they come to install it and it doesn't fit? Plus, it would be better for the environment and our bank account. Each time I go on the Internet and look at microwave prices, my eyes are drawn to the new ovens and range tops, both of which we could use. Ours are at least 15 years old, and I'm not certain how much longer they can last.

But I shall cool my heels and wait for my hubby to figure things out. If he can repair the microwave, I'll be happy. If he decides he can't fix it, I'll approach the subject of new appliances (and be happy with whatever we can afford).

Here is where marriages sink or swim – in the art of compromise. Dale will find a way to get to the microwave, and I'll take deep breaths and find new ways to reheat leftovers.

How long do you think it takes to heat soup with the hair dryer?

COOKING THE BOOKS

For someone who isn't a very good cook, I love cookbooks. Actually, it's not only cookbooks—I love recipes. I have about 30 large books, a handful of the little Reader's Digest-sized pamphlets, a binder filled with pages torn from magazines, and an old plastic box of index cards.

The books range from the generic, Betty Crocker, to the particular, such as Mexican Cooking (yes, for Dummies). The pamphlets are very specific and give recipes, not just for appetizers, but Appetizers in 10 Minutes. The index cards contain no-fail dishes I've cooked for years, like Texas chili, carrot cake, and my grandmother's banana bread.

With all of these ideas at my fingertips, you'd think the last words I'd ever mutter are, "I don't know what to make for dinner tonight." You'd be wrong.

My family is not picky. Dale will eat anything, although I've learned, over the 17 years of our marriage, that he doesn't care as much for bland food with cream sauces as he does spicy foods. But even if I cook something a little calm, his theory is everything's better with a little Tabasco and black pepper.

I used to say Marcus was a picky eater when he was younger, but my friend described it as being "specific", which sounds better. He specifically ate pasta, rice, and vegetables, and avoided meat at all costs. Before you congratulate me on having a boy who ate broccoli, let me remind you, they don't serve that at baseball games, Chuck E. Cheese, or KinderCare.

He still managed to get enough protein into his body to grow up, and he eventually grew out of his specific eating habits. I'm happy to report that he now eats whatever I cook.

So why aren't I preparing some of the delicious dishes I see in my wealth of cookbooks? Part of it could be that I have had cooking errors; I follow the directions and it still doesn't look like the picture. After a major disaster, my confidence is eroded and I return to my standard meal of broiled meat, rice, and steamed vegetables. Part of it is definitely that, although a recipe looks good at first glance, a closer inspection reveals food I either don't want to eat (veal, for example) or a preparation method I've never tried (see confidence, above).

A greater part of why I'm not using my cookbooks for my family's greater culinary good has to do with our schedule. Each time I find a new recipe, purchase the items at the grocery store and make plans to serve it, our week goes haywire. In the last two weeks, we've been home for dinner maybe three times. Marcus has had practice or Dale had to work late or I went to a meeting, and then there were Marcus' last-minute invitations to awards ceremonies, all of which threw my dinner plans into chaos.

After a few weeks like that, I'm afraid to buy anything that might spoil in less than a month.

I've decided to live with the dining turmoil until school is out, and try new recipes during the summer, when we shouldn't be running so amok. In the meantime, Marcus and Dale don't seem to mind the meat, rice, veggie regimen. Every once in awhile, I sneak in a potato, but Marcus told me I don't need to do that very often.

"Your rice-to-potato ratio is good, Mom," he said.

Maybe I should continue to cook the same meals every night and just read the cookbooks for fun. After all, I love a good mystery.

WHEN IT RAINS...

I was pleased to read about the $5 stimulus coupons the city of Placentia gave out a few weeks ago. Although I didn't receive one, I still thought it was a good idea. We all need a boost during this rough economy, even if it's just lifting our spirits to see our cities trying to be helpful.

Our household is hanging on, mostly due to Dale's job as an engineer, but I'm looking closer at my purchases and asking myself if I really need the brand name pasta, or the better cut of meat. It's not like I usually run through the aisles, throwing money around on caviar and filet mignon, but I'm thinking about every purchase a little bit harder and passing up what I don't truly need.

Too bad my house is not cooperating. Last week, I reported the death of the microwave; after careful examination, Dale agreed I should go buy a new one. Microwaves have gotten fairly cheap, so I wasn't too concerned.

Then on Friday, I unloaded the dishwasher and got a bad surprise—there was standing water in the bottom. I looked under the sink for something to bail out the water and discovered that it was wet under there, too. Not "standing puddles, obviously leaking" wet, just wet. I found a cup, and, after bailing out the dishwasher, I washed the day's dirty dishes by hand.

I had just finished the last pan when Dale walked in and announced the water heater was broken. At this point, my mind went into complete denial.

"But I just used the hot water to wash the dishes," I told him.

"Not that kind of broken. It's leaking." He sounded a little churlish.

At that point, we had a disastrous conversation, where I didn't want to believe my house was falling apart and he was upset about my unwillingness to accept that, not only was the water heater dead, the shut-off valve didn't work and he had turned off the water to the entire house. In his defense, I hadn't told him about the dishwasher or the sink leakage yet.

So we spent the rest of Friday and most of Saturday with the water turned off, only turning it on for brief periods when we had to brush teeth and clean up. By the afternoon, Dale had managed to make the shut-off valve work, so at least we had steady, cold water.

On Sunday, I went to Home Depot and purchased a new water heater, which they would deliver and install on Monday. I came home feeling a little better. I also felt a little poorer; water heaters are not cheap.

That's when the bees showed up. Marcus announced there was a bee in the house.

"Actually, there are several," he said.

He was right. It turns out, we had a squadron of scout bees inspecting our chimney and leaking into our home from small spaces in the closed flue. At least, that's what the Bee Man said when he came to round them up. The good news was that it wasn't a hive. The bad news was that all the scouts would lead Her Hiney, the Queen, to our chimney in the next couple of days. So now my fireplace is blocked with a trash bag taped to the brick. It's a new décor: Early American Crazy Lady.

The bee man felt so bad about my water heater, he gave me a discount on his service. It was nice to have a little financial stimulus. My house has stimulated me quite enough this week.

TORTURED DRIVING

Summer is approaching, and I had high hopes that Marcus would be nearly finished with his driving instruction. It's been almost three months since he got his learner's permit, and almost two since he had his first lesson with the instructor. He's come a long way since those first few days of gutter-hugging, but he's not quite ready for his next lesson yet. Especially since his next lesson will take him onto the freeway.

Dale and I are trying to make certain Marcus gets a lot of practice to build his confidence. We make him drive us around town on as many errands as possible. Sometimes Dale goes above and beyond in his attempt to give our son plenty of hours behind the wheel.

A couple of weeks ago, Marcus decided he needed a haircut. For some reason, he can never simply say, "Mom, I think I'll need a haircut soon. Could you make an appointment for sometime in the next two weeks?"

Instead, he tells me, "Mom, I need a haircut. How soon can you make the appointment?" By the time he says this, Dale has also been snapping at my heels about our son's hair, so the entire household leads me to believe the haircut must happen immediately or the world as we know it will end.

I must learn how to do this, because no matter how impatient I sound when I'm asking them to pick up their clutter, neither of my guys see global implications in my request for a clean house.

When Marcus announced his need for shorter hair on Friday evening, I asked Dale what the Saturday schedule was like. He and Marcus were going to run in a charity 5K in the morning, so he said the afternoon looked free. I called Larry on Saturday morning to see if he had anything available. He had a one o'clock appointment, so I called Dale and left a message.

At noon, Dale returned my call. "It depends on traffic," he told me. "We're just leaving now."

"Leaving from where?" For some reason, I thought the event had been local.

"The Coliseum."

I called Larry and gave him the update. "Not a problem," he said.

Unfortunately, a secretary's work is never done. Around 12:30, Dale called me again. "I don't think we'll make it back until at least 1:30."

"Is traffic that bad?" I asked.

"No. Marcus is driving."

In the movies, this would be the place where the camera zooms in on my horrified face as the music blares. I pictured the two of them on the I-110, driving 45 miles per hour, in the gutter. I called Larry again.

"I can still wait," he told me. "Or would you rather re-schedule?"

"I'd rather re-schedule," I said. "You see, Marcus is driving—from the Coliseum. Let's not make him rush."

As I returned home, they were also pulling into the driveway, Marcus behind the wheel. For someone who spent a few hours running in the bright sun, he looked remarkably pale. I learned they stayed off the freeway and took surface streets all the way, surface streets with lots of traffic.

"Such a long time, so many cars," was all he would say as he collapsed on the couch.

I've told him to tell me when he's ready for the next lesson, but at this point, I don't know when that will happen. I'm not certain which freeway his instructor, Don, will take him on, but I'm hoping it will be the one with the widest lanes at the quietest hour.

THE FOUNTAIN OF YUCK

When it comes to parenthood, home ownership and life in general, I spend half my time as a smart cookie and the other half as a poster child for "Don't Do It Like This." This week, my face was definitely on the poster.

It began when the toilet in Marcus' bathroom began running. The first time I heard it, it sounded odd. There is a normal sound of a tank filling that you get used to, and this wasn't it. I mentioned this to Dale.

"Just jiggle the handle," he told me.

I did, but it didn't help, so I removed the tank lid and saw water pouring from the cap at the top of the fill valve. I pressed down on the cap and the water stopped, so I made a mental note of "one more thing to try when a toilet is running."

The next morning, after everyone had left, I decided to see if the toilet had somehow fixed itself. It hadn't. Water was pouring into the tank, at what sounded like an alarming force. Tentatively, I lifted the lid.

Again, the water was running from the cap, but there appeared to be more coming out than the previous day. I pressed down on the cap to stop it and… the cap came off.

Actually, it didn't pop away from the valve, but I could feel it under my palm, ready to fly to the ceiling as soon as I took my hand away. I pressed down harder, twisted the cap left and right, but it was no use. As soon as I lifted my hand, I knew what would happen. I'd have a geyser in the bathroom.

Holding the cap down with one hand, I reached down to the shut-off valve with the other. That's when I discovered a harsh fact of home ownership: old shut-off valves are impossible to turn. So there I was, like the little boy trying to hold up the dam with one finger, with no one at home to help me.

I considered several options. One was to find a tool to turn the shut-off valve. Another was to call Dale or the plumber for help and stand with my hand on the cap until they arrived. Crying could accompany either choice.

In the end, I opted for Solution 1. I lined the floor with towels, then quickly slipped the tank lid on. I heard the cap hit the lid and saw the water pour down the tank. My plan hit a snag when I raced into the garage and couldn't find a wrench. In desperation I ran outside to the main valve and shut off all water to the house.

While I mopped up the mess, I tried to figure out what to do. Should I call the plumber or wait for Dale? No matter what, I vowed to have a talk with my son about cleaning his bathroom more often.

I took one more look at the tank. The cap lay at the bottom, so I picked it up and examined it. It had some threads that matched the threads at the top of the fill valve. I placed it on the valve and turned, and it locked.

After I replaced the lid and put a bucket underneath the toilet, I went back outside, turned on the water, and ran into the house. The tank filled gently, then stopped. Victory!

I was tired but proud of myself. I may have started the day as a poster child, but I ended it as a smart, if slightly soggy, cookie.

TRANSLATING ACROSS THE GENDERS

It's official. Men speak a different language and I don't have a translator. Oh, I can talk to them about life in general. But when I need to exchange important information, it all falls apart.

I experienced this recently with both my husband and son, kind of like having the cell phone and landline die.

It started when Dale caught a cold. He began complaining of a sore throat, and then draped himself across the couch, where he remained motionless for the rest of the evening. I raided our medicine cabinets and brought out various pain relievers and cold medications for him to take.

The following day, I stopped at the store for milk, so I called to see if he needed anything else.

"I don't know," he said. "What do we have at home?"

"All we have is what I left on the coffee table for you last night."

He was silent for such a long time, I thought I'd lost the connection. "I have a sore throat," he finally told me.

The medicine aisle didn't have anything specific to sore throats, apart from lozenges. I selected a couple of brands and figured he could also take an analgesic for the inflammation. When I arrived home, I told him what I'd purchased as I unpacked.

"I have a fever," he said.

I could have used this information earlier, if only I'd known that "sore throat" was code for "just get me some kind of cold and flu medication." Our language gap kept me from getting him something more useful than honey-lemon drops.

I thought perhaps I'd have a chance of communicating with Marcus, since I've been talking to him since birth, and he's been returning the favor for a few years. But last Monday, he showed signs of maturing into a man.

A man I can't understand.

He's finishing his internship at the recording studio, and has been working mostly Sunday and Monday. Typically, he goes in at four or five o'clock and finishes around midnight or one in the morning. Sometimes I pick him up, and sometimes one of the guys brings him home.

This past Monday, I drove him to the studio after school. I didn't expect to see him before midnight, so I sent him a text message at twelve thirty.

"Home soon?" I wrote.

Ten minutes later, I received this response: "Yep."

I sat in the bedroom chair, in my jeans and t-shirt, watching the Food Network, and waiting for the call to pick him up. As I waited, I dozed off and on, until my neck ached from the odd position. At one o'clock, I sent him another text, and then curled up on the bed, still in my clothes, waiting. This time he didn't answer.

I tried again at one thirty, with no response. I called him at two, but it rolled over to voice mail, so I sent another text: "Call me!!!" I guess I thought the phone would vibrate more with those extra exclamation points.

By two-thirty, I was ready to hop in the car and hunt him down. I tried calling one more time. This time, he answered.

"Where are you?" I asked.

"In my room, asleep," he mumbled.

Apparently, his first answer of "Yep" meant "Yes, I got a ride home and will be there in about ten minutes." He had slipped into the house while I napped.

We talked about it the next day, and he promised to communicate better. In the meantime, I'm going to the library to see if they have a Man-to-Woman Dictionary. I need one.

MY MINIVAN'S CUTE NEW SHOES

As much as I adore my mechanic, Allen, I hate having my car serviced. One reason is pure girly vanity. A new outfit usually results in compliments, but no one ever says, "Wow, did you get an oil change? Your car sounds great."

The other reason is cost, which seems to increase as my car gets older. Now that my minivan is twelve years old and has traveled 185,000 miles, I'm pretty sure Allen has to scour antique stores for parts. It's even possible that time travel is involved. He tries to keep my bill low, but those stores on the Orange Circle aren't cheap.

All of which is why I may have waited a little when I first felt my brakes get squishy. And, when my car began to shudder at sudden stops, I might have been too busy to take it in for servicing. It took my son's scolding look, during a practice drive, when he said, "You got the brakes done, right," and I answered, "No," to make me drive to Hale's Automotive on Monday.

The diagnosis was what I expected; this part was worn and that part was leaking, and I needed an oil change. Then Allen made that face he makes when he's going to discuss my car's quality of life.

"Your front struts are leaking," he told me. My blank expression encouraged him to continue. "Over time, your front tires will stop hugging the road. They're already starting to show a funny wear pattern from not being held down consistently."

He did the math to give me an estimate, with and without the struts. Either way, it wasn't pretty.

"How long do you plan to keep the van?" he asked.

I thought, *I'm not sure I planned to keep the van this long.*

I explained that Marcus has one more year of high school, which means one more year of me chauffeuring and chaperoning the choir. I need a vehicle that can shuttle these kids around. Once he's off to college and it's just me and Dale and the animals, I can get a smaller car, one that can hold me, my saddle, and my books (we'll throw Dale in there, too).

"It's got to get through another year."

Allen made that face again. "If you told me you weren't going to keep it, I'd say skip the repairs to the struts. But if you're keeping it, and especially if you're driving kids around in it..." He left the sentence unfinished, but we both knew what came next.

I paid the money and all of the repairs were performed.

Now that my mechanic's given it a clean bill of health, I'm starting to think about keeping the minivan even longer, and giving it to Marcus when he goes to school. After all, it's big enough to carry all of his musical equipment, and even move him in and out of a dorm room every year.

I explained the plan to Marcus, thinking he'd love to have a van to haul his friends around. Surprisingly, he wasn't too crazy about having a Mom Car. I even offered to have it painted an interesting color (it's currently white).

His response was immediate. "Um, nah, that's okay."

In the meantime, I will continue to enjoy my senior auto-citizen. At least Marcus noticed a difference after all the money I spent.

"The brakes aren't as squishy, and there's no shuddering," he said as he drove us down Alta Vista Street.

It's not exactly the same as being told my new shoes are cute, but I'll take it.

MY SON, THE FASHIONISTA

I am writing this a week before school starts, and Marcus enters his senior year of high school at Valencia. This milestone has made me more nostalgic than usual. I can't be the only parent this happens to, and I hope we're not all on the road at the same time, reminiscing about the past.

It started with senior pictures. As I watched Marcus hold his oversized Velcro tux jacket with one hand while he tipped his chin and smiled for the camera, I flashed back to the days when he brought the folder home with pictures they'd taken at school. Like Forrest Gump said, it was like a box of chocolates: I never knew what we were going to get. Would his shirt be clean? How about his face?

The only surprise this time was that, although the photographer managed to squeeze the graduation cap onto Marcus' large hair, somehow he made it poof out to the side unevenly. As a result, all of the cap and gown pictures look like his hair is trying to escape. In retrospect, as a Valtech student, Marcus won't even be wearing a blue gown, so we might have wasted that pose.

After the pictures, I started to think about getting ready for school, in terms of clothes. In the old days, this meant going through my son's closet to get rid of anything that didn't fit him, then shopping for new. When he was very young, I shopped without him. At Morse Elementary, there was a uniform of polo shirts and pants, which made it easy.

As he turned the corner toward puberty, I thought he might have an opinion about what he wore. He didn't, but I took him to Mervyn's, and Kids R Us, trying to find shirts and pants he liked. His response to shopping was to adhere his feet to the tile and force me to drag him down each aisle.

My response to that was to refer to him as SlugBoy in one of my columns—it was the only time he's ever complained about something I wrote.

Last year, I accompanied him to Old Navy, showed him where his size was, and told him to pick out what he wanted. He rolled his eyes, shrugged, and wandered about as if he was being led to the noose. Finally, he arrived at the cash register, with some shorts and a pair of pants, I think.

This year, he approached me one morning as I sat working at my computer.

"Alex and I are going shopping at Kohl's. We've decided to set a new fashion on campus."

He stood there.

"You need money?"

He nodded, so I gave him some cash, and the boys were off. Over the next hour, I got pictures of his purchases, sent to my cell phone. Not only did his shopping trip cost me $100, I'll probably be paying for it in my cell phone bill this month.

While he was gone, I thought about my little boy, who wore his hair super short and didn't care what color or style his clothes were. He'd been replaced by some teenager with facial hair and a Jimi Hendrix Afro, who was rummaging through racks of purple shirts.

When did that happen?

So if you see me around and I look a little dazed, I'm probably thinking about a baby I used to hold, a boy I used to dress, and the young man I'm about to unleash upon the world.

I can't be the only one doing this, can I?

BIRTHDAYS DON'T CARE

Dale gave me his cold last week. I'm not complaining, but usually I get nicer gifts from him.

Watching his symptoms, I tried to find out if it was a cold or swine flu. After seventeen years, I should know not to ask my husband how he feels, yet I cannot resist.

"Do you have a headache? Body aches? Fever?"

The responses were a shrug, a head shake, and "not anymore."

When I'm sick, I tell my family exactly what is wrong with me. I can remain pretty chipper about it until someone asks me to do anything unplanned, at which point I become Mega-Whiney Woman.

Dale's way may be better.

He tried not to give me his cold. There was no close contact, and he even slept in the guest bedroom. In the end, the germs didn't care about our precautions; they hunted me down like a pack of coyotes. Dale might as well have slept in our bed and coughed in my face.

All I could think of when I awoke on Sunday morning with a scratchy throat was to stuff myself full of water, drugs, and Vitamin C. I needed to get on a plane in four days, and did not want to be flying with a head full of cotton.

In addition, Dale left for Arizona on a three-week business trip, so I had to make arrangements for Marcus. At seventeen, he could theoretically stay home. Valencia High School is within walking distance; I could pack the house with food and he'd be fine.

When I offered him this option, he told me he preferred to stay with his friend, Alex. This meant I had to stop the newspaper, board the dog, and make a list of things Marcus needed to do every day.

Between Dale's trip and Marcus staying with Alex, I had plenty of unplanned events to make me one whiney gal.

In the midst of our chaos, Marcus had a birthday. He requested a low-key celebration of dinner with friends. Since his birthday was on Monday, I thought we could go to his favorite restaurant, Bubba Gump's, on Sunday, before Dale left for Arizona.

On Saturday, I asked Marcus if he'd talked to Alex about dinner.

"I can't go," he said. "I gotta work."

"It's your birthday, and you're working an internship. Can't you ask them for the evening off?"

Marcus looked stricken. While I applauded his sense of responsibility, I tried to talk him into calling his boss and explaining.

"Alex can't go either," he told me.

Dale and I gave him his card and present Monday morning, and I assumed we'd celebrate his birthday later, perhaps when Dale came home. I also assumed I'd be able to rest all evening and kick this cold. I was still relaxing in my PJs when Marcus came home from school.

"Are we going to dinner tonight?" he asked. "This is the only night Alex can do it."

I started to explain how awful I felt and that I just wanted to curl up in a ball and sleep without coughing. But his face was so earnest, and he had been so helpful recently, I couldn't let him down.

"Give me a little time to clean up," I told him.

I took him and Alex to a fine meal at Bubba Gump's. He gorged himself on seafood and thanked me for the iTunes cards he received. We went home, where I collapsed in bed, while my son scampered off to purchase more music.

He's right about the cards. They're a much better gift than a cold.

BONDING AND VENTING

I know I complain about my family's lack of communication. There are days when Marcus seems to be writing a book, on how to live on one syllable a day. As for my husband, in his defense, Dale may have grown tired of my inability to hear his soft, deep voice, so he possibly limits his words to the important ones, like, "we need milk," or "the dryer's on fire."

Sometimes, however, I am treated to a plethora of words. All I have to do is figure out whether they're pointed toward me.

Dale has spent a few evenings telling me about the softball game his team played, the 3rd graders he is coaching in basketball, or the latest Survivor episode. I am thrilled to know these details. It's not really a conversation, but I listen for any opportunity to ask a question or make a suggestion.

He doesn't seem to need questions, and he really doesn't want suggestions. I keep reading experts who say that the problem with communications between men and women is that men only talk when they want to solve a problem, and women talk to vent and don't want any advice.

I don't know who the experts are, but I think they've got it backwards. How do they explain all those women's letters to Dear Abby?

Marcus is also getting into the act. Before he auditioned for the Southern California Vocal Association Honor Choir this year, he had a few words to say.

"I don't know whether to audition as a tenor or a bass this year," he told me.

As the mom, I thought I was supposed to offer suggestions. "Could you sing a song that covers both ranges? That way, if they had enough tenors, they could consider you as a bass."

"No, there's no such song. Besides, they don't do that. They only consider you for what you put on the form." After shooting down my idea, he added, "I may not even get in this year. My voice isn't that remarkable, and I don't think my sight reading is strong."

"I guess it's possible," I said. "But you've been in the Honor Choir for two years, and last year you made All State. They probably know you by now, know your work ethic and your abilities."

"That's not the way it works, Mom. You can make it one year and not the next."

Finally, I asked, "Do you want any advice or suggestions, or are you just venting?"

"Just venting."

"Oh, then go ahead," I encouraged him. "Talk away."

But the moment was gone. He had nothing left to say about getting into Honor Choir, not even when he was accepted into it. When I congratulated him, it was apparently one of his word-rationing days, so he shrugged his shoulders.

By contrast, I talk a lot at home, about everything. I give information, I direct my family toward tasks that need to be done, and I ask questions in the hope that someday someone may actually answer them.

Early in our marriage, I came home with an engineering problem on my mind. I delivered a soliloquy about what had happened at work, while Dale listened.

"Am I supposed to do something with this information?" he asked.

"No. I'm just bonding with you."

He looked as though he'd been given the grandest *aha* moment ever. "Bonding! That's what you've been doing all this time, with all the talking."

Yes, I've been bonding, and they've been venting. Whatever they call it, I'll be happy for any syllables they throw my way.

LEARNING FROM MISTAKES

My dog does not understand cause and effect. If, for example, he eats something that makes him sick, he will still try to eat it again, even if it sent him to the hospital the first time. The cat is no better; she will try to jump on the counter 51 times, even after I've blocked 50 attempts.

By contrast, I learn from my mistakes, which is why I no longer eat Brussels sprouts. This is what separates us from the rest of the animal kingdom.

Well, that and blushing.

Over my lifetime, I've learned not to do a lot of things. My recent plumbing problem taught me, when I hear a hissing noise coming from the toilet, to turn off the water before I lift the lid to investigate. I no longer put leftover rice in the garbage disposal, after crawling under the sink to clean the clogged trap—twice. And, it only took me one season and a few wasted hours of listening to bad singers and mean judges, to kick the American Idol habit.

In doing laundry every week for Marcus and Dale, I've also learned to check pockets before I throw anything into the washing machine. In addition to laundering Dale's wallet, I have been unpleasantly surprised by the extra designs made by stray ink pens left in his slacks. As for Marcus, we won't talk about his "crayons, bugs, and rock collecting" phase. Of course, the upside to checking pockets is that I keep any money I find. Someday, I'll retire as a rich woman.

A few years ago, I accidentally washed and dried Dale's cell phone. He had left it in his cargo shorts, buried in one of the thousand pockets. I discovered my error when I heard the ominous thump-thump of something that doesn't belong in the dryer.

The young man at the Verizon store had nothing but bad news for me that day. Not only was the phone completely destroyed, I had to pay full price for a new one. You see, I hadn't bought the insurance, since the last time I carried insurance on Dale's phone, it didn't end well. Dale lost the phone, the insurance company wanted him to file a police report, and he refused, saying the phone wasn't stolen.

I didn't see anything to be gained by insuring the next phone, until I pulled it out of the dryer.

After that experience, I did insure all future phones, and I diligently checked all pockets… until last weekend, when Dale walked into the family room.

"I need a new phone," he told me. "You washed and dried mine in my pocket."

Not just any phone, this was Dale's Blackberry. Once again, I had missed one of the many nooks and crannies of my husband's cargo pants. This time, however, it was buried so deeply I didn't even hear it clunking around in the machine.

I filed the insurance report online. I loved the simplicity of their question: "Did the phone come in contact with liquid of any kind?" There was no need to explain, no blame to be placed on me for not finding the phone, or Dale for leaving it there. It got wet, so they would replace it.

The new phone arrived quickly, and is currently being charged and readied for service. In the meantime, although washing a phone once every four years isn't a bad record, I've decided to take steps to learn from my mistake and ensure this never happens again.

From now on, I'm banning cargo pants.

CALL ME IMMOVEABLE

I've been hearing a lot of talk about real estate lately. Friends and family are selling houses, buying houses, or talking about what kind of house they'll buy when they sell the one they own now.

My friends, Niki and Dave, have decided to get a larger place, one that's a little more equidistant between their respective jobs. Surprisingly, they were able to sell their home very quickly. Partly this was due to their upgrades, especially in the kitchen. Everyone likes to imagine that they would become master chefs if they only had granite countertops and stainless steel appliances.

After all, Stouffer's Chicken Pot Pies taste much better when they're cooked in your state-of-the-art convection oven, don't they?

In addition, my friends "staged" their house, a practice so common that it's almost a physical law. Apparently, if you move everything out of your house that reminds potential buyers you still live there, they can imagine themselves sitting in your leather chaise, watching your flat-screen TV.

Of course, if they buy your house, they will be moving in the plaid recliner with duct tape and the 20-year old RCA console. But let them dream.

I tell people that Dale and I are never moving. After changing addresses every five years or so, I'm simply tired of the experience. Unlike childbirth, time does not erase the pain of packing and unpacking boxes.

In each of my many moves, I've promised to organize and purge items as I packed, but I always ended up throwing everything into random boxes. I then promised to sort it out as I unpacked. This also proved impossible; unwanted things ended up in the garage, or stuffed in the back of the linen closet.

At each new location, I managed to accrue a few more items that seemed necessary when I bought them, but eventually fell into the Unwanted Bin with the other junk.

Basically, I live like a goldfish. I always grow to the size of my container.

We moved into our current home 14 years ago, from about 1200 square feet, to 2600 square feet. We didn't even pretend to purge. Things that should have been discarded from the previous home were free to roam about the abundant closets, as well as the spare bedrooms and the shelves in the garage. Over the years, they've been joined by more stuff.

Let's face it, I no longer have a residence. I have a Junk Sanctuary.

If Dale and I had to stage our house to sell it, we'd have to rent a storage space to put all of our personal things. I can guarantee that the rental would become a secondary home to the Carlines' pile of junk, like a satellite location.

We'd also have to update a few things, like our kitchen. Although we've gotten a new roof, windows, and exterior painting in the last few years, most of our home improvement projects involve changing light bulbs, and taking down the Christmas decorations before Halloween. I'd love to have a pretty kitchen with new cabinets and shiny appliances, but it won't improve my cooking.

Besides, if we update the house, why would I want to sell it?

I've told Dale there are only two conditions under which I'd move. One is if we're so rich, someone else packs it, moves it, and unpacks it, while we hang out at the Hilton in our fluffy robes. The other is if we are so poor, we're on the street with our shopping carts.

Until then, don't bother me with anything in between.

WHEN TOYS TALK BACK

I love technology. We have so many entertaining toys these days.

Many years ago, I got a job as a photographer's assistant for a mall Santa Claus (no, I didn't have to dress like an elf) and had to attend a training session in Chicago. The hotel's elevators announced each floor, using a female voice that was soothing, yet creepy. Perhaps the creepy factor was in the way the doors would not open until the floor number was announced in that slow, calm Voice.

The first day, it was a marvel of technology. On the second day, it was irritating. By the time I left for home, I believed the Voice was an actual entity, who held us hostage until we agreed to its demands ("yes, Ma'am, it IS the third floor").

From that moment, I began seeing personalities in every piece of equipment that spoke, and I can't seem to stop.

Dale's car is equipped with a GPS navigation system. Directions are crooned to him by a soft, feminine voice he has named "Lola," after his boyhood crush, Lola Falana. I admit to some feelings of irritation and perhaps jealousy when she is instructing us to our destination; she always wants to take the busiest freeways, and the most convoluted side streets to arrive at an address. Dale thinks she is a computer-generated voice, programmed into a system that doesn't account for traffic reports, or whether the longer, straightforward route is better than a shorter zig-zag.

Engineers are often grounded in reality like that. It's a compromise I've had to make.

My minivan is too old to have been GPS-equipped, and I have not felt the need to purchase one, mostly because I don't want to hang a bunch of stuff on the dashboard of my car, just to bring it into the 21st century. I have my Thomas Guide, I get detailed directions on MapQuest prior to any large trip, and recently, I've discovered the navigation system on my cell phone.

My phone has a feature called VZ Navigator. Not only can it give me directions, it can find businesses of just about any type and then tell me how to get to them. Again, these instructions are given to me by a female voice. I'm guessing that someone did market research and decided that no one liked having a man order them around, but we wouldn't mind if a woman could "suggest" a right turn here and there.

It didn't take me long to imagine the woman behind the voice on my phone. Actually, I've decided there are two women giving me directions, Wanda and Justine. Wanda is the clear-headed career gal, who can tell me when I'm approaching a turn, or a traffic incident. Justine is her drunken sister, who is barely hanging onto her job of pronouncing street names.

For example, they were directing me to Irvine last weekend, and Wanda told me plainly, "Prepare to turn left, onto—" She then turned to Justine, who stammered, "MAG-Arthrrr Bull-vard."

Often, the street name has been so mangled I have to glance down at the phone to read it. I think Wanda may be enabling her sister, and I'm concerned.

Before any of you become concerned for my mental health, I don't truly think there are two women lurking about in my cell phone.

I only think it's fun to play with my toys.

CHECKING UNDER THE HOOD

This week, I got my yearly checkup and mammogram. When I made my appointments last year, I discovered that two or three years had elapsed since my last "yearly" visit, so I made certain my computer sent me a reminder this time.

I also made my appointments for the same week, Tuesday and Wednesday. I figured, if I've got to be poked, prodded and scrutinized, why not make a week of it?

My first date was with Dr. Jerry Thanos, who has been my doctor for years. He and his brother, Dr. Nick, delivered Marcus. Complications had required a C-section, so while I was in a semi-fog, they worked to make certain Dale and I took home a healthy baby.

This year, I sat in a waiting room filled with expectant mothers, feeling like the odd mom out. Most of them were alone, but a couple had their husbands along, so I didn't feel nearly as out of place as the men looked.

One couple had brought their baby for an in-patient procedure. Dad found it difficult to sit still. He talked on the phone, he asked the desk if they could change the TV channel, all while Mom cooed to their newborn. I enjoyed watching the mother try to ward off any baby whimpers, remembering those days when I was a new mom who didn't want her kiddo to cry.

If there was one thing I wished I could have shared with these women, it's that I never knew how little control I had over life until I had a baby.

Eventually, I was ushered into the little room and given directions about which way the paper gown should open. Except they no longer have paper gowns. They have paper blouses. For a woman who spent years in the relative security of the knee-length robe, the little paper blouse seems like the definition of exposure. I'm short, and the top ends well above my waist. I can't imagine the lack of coverage for a taller gal.

We're also given a paper sheet to cover our lower halves, but there's still an area of midriff that makes me feel like my outfit is too small. As I grow older, I'm actually considering buying my own paper gowns to take to these appointments. I've spent a lot of years having uncomfortable exams - do I really need to feel unfashionable, too?

They used to have blouses at the St. Jude Breast Center. I can understand the use of blouses for a mammogram. You only undress from the waist up, unless you forgot your appointment and wore a dress that day. In the old center, they had a little dressing area in the same room as the equipment, so a dress snafu was not a problem.

The new location has full-on dressing rooms, complete with seating, a mirror, clothes hangers, and even a can of spray-on deodorant. It's a lot of fuss to wear a blouse for ten minutes of pictures.

Although now they don't have blouses, they have capes. Spacious cotton capes in an array of flowery prints, they either make you feel like a superhero or a queen, depending upon your mood. I don't know about anyone else, but hugging a cold machine and trying to relax while certain body parts are being flattened like roadkill does not make me feel either all-powerful or royal.

In addition to the paper dress, perhaps I should get my own cape, too, a red one with an ermine collar. Add a tiara, and my doctor visits would be so festive, I probably wouldn't need a reminder.

SPORTS BY OSMOSIS

One of the things Marcus had to cut out of his senior year was sports. Music is now the dominant force in his life, leaving no time for other activities, although Dale will probably make him play a few basketball games on his spring league.

I often feel a twinge of sadness that he had to abandon soccer. Playing soccer and basketball was an important way for him to spend time with Dale. There are many sporting events on our TV, but Marcus is not interested in watching them, so my guys are typically not bonding over the Laker game or Monday Night Football.

Soccer and basketball have been Marcus' main sports, but he has tried tennis, roller hockey, and of course, horseback riding. When he was six, we tried to sign him up for a baseball clinic, but he declined.

"At my age, I need a more team-oriented sport," he told me.

We had no rebuttal.

For some reason, we never tried to sign him up for football. Perhaps it's because none of the city recreation services offered it. I admit a certain bias against football, because I hate to watch high school boys practicing in August in full gear. Call me a mom, but it can only end in fainting—either by the boys on the field or the moms when their sons get in the car after practice.

As far as I know, Marcus has never played football, and I've never seen him watch a game. He's gone to some Valencia games, but I can't swear that he paid attention to what happened on the field. After all, I used to go to my high school games and I was always too busy talking to my friends.

So imagine my surprise when Marcus sat, by himself, and watched the Super Bowl on Sunday. I had originally called him in to watch the Who perform the halftime show. There was about two minutes left in the half, so I thought he'd wander in and out of the room until he heard a familiar chord. Instead, he sat down.

I began hearing phrases from him, like, "same play as last," and "nice shotgun formation." He corrected my comment about stopping the clock while they moved the chains. He said the Saints should stop trying to run the ball and pass more. He talked just like… Dale.

At last, I couldn't stand it. "How do you know all this stuff?" I asked. "I have never seen you watch a single game of football."

"It's a manly thing, Mom. We all know it."

I thought I had found some secret link in the male DNA chain, until later, when I was pointing out the commentators in the studio.

"That's Dan Marino," I said. "He was the quarterback for the Dolphins."

"I know who Dan Marino is."

"How can you know that? He retired years ago."

Marcus shrugged. "I saw him on a weight loss commercial."

We watched Pete and Roger do their medley, wondered if that was still Zach Starkey behind the drums, and I left to finish my paperwork in the dining room. I assumed Marcus would return to his room and do whatever it is that he does. Sometimes I hear music. Sometimes I hear a video game. I never hear the sound of the vacuum cleaner.

But this time, all I heard were shouts coming from the room where the football game was playing. It was Marcus' voice, with Dale's words coming out of it.

I guess my guys have been bonding while I wasn't looking.

FOR THE LOVE OF GOD, FIX THE A/C!

I don't care whether it's the heat or the humidity. Once the temperature outside reaches one hundred degrees, it's officially too darned hot outside. Good thing we all have air conditioning to escape the oven known as southern California.

Unless we don't.

As luck would have it, our air conditioner broke on one of the triple-digit weekends. Nothing in my house ever breaks when it would be convenient to call a repairman, or when we can live without it for a few days while we call for repairs.

Whatever it is, it breaks when we need it most.

The good news is, I didn't really notice the air conditioning was broken until Saturday evening. I was at the ranch in the morning, sweating profusely, then ran home and cleaned up before meeting some friends for dinner and a movie. The bedroom seemed a little warm, but that part of the house always seems warm. And the family room felt cool, as usual.

I was having a turkey burger with my girlfriends when Dale sent me a text. "AC not coming on. That is why house so hot or did you not notice?"

Um, no, guess I didn't.

I noticed on Sunday, though, when I spent the day laying in front of a fan, too hot to even put on decent clothes and go to the mall, or the movies, or anywhere with cold air blasting through the room. Instead, I went to the Internet, searching for a repair service.

I've had a few bad repair experiences. Okay, a lot of them. Typically, I expect to call two repair shops, because the first one will not show up, will lie to me about why, and then will be deafened by the sound of me, pounding the phone on the table. The second repairman will show up and charge me an arm and both legs, which I will pay because I desperately need to use whatever's broken.

Let's just say I was praying for an appliance repair miracle.

What I found was a site that took my name, address, and problem description, then sent me the names of three local services with links to their websites, ratings, etc. One of the services was rated significantly higher than the others, so I planned to call that one on Monday.

After all, I may have been miserable, but I wasn't going to pay extra for emergency repairs.

Color me surprised when my first selection called me on Sunday. He explained he got an email notification that I needed service, and could be at my house between 8 and 10 Monday morning. I agreed, then sat back and waited for disaster.

At 8:30 on Monday, a nice, if slightly scary, man with a Russian accent and a scar on his face knocked on my door. The first thing he did was chide me for not changing the air filter more often.

I have a hard time remembering to clean the top of the refrigerator because I don't see it. What are the chances I'll decide to locate the correct wrench to open the furnace and pull out the filter?

Next, he moved to the air conditioning unit. It took him five minutes to pronounce the starter dead. A new starter, and a couple of pounds of Freon from him, and a check for a reasonable amount from me, and I had cold air pumping through my vents again. He was gone in less than an hour.

The whole thing lifted my spirits for the rest of the day. I guess, even in stifling heat, there's room for a miracle.

OUT OF CONTROL AND PROUD OF IT

A reader emailed me with a question regarding a recent column I wrote, about my doctor visits. I had written, "I never knew how little control I had over life until I had a baby." The reader is planning to be a mom herself, and perhaps misinterpreted the statement as an indication that I got more control of life once I became a mother.

Let me clarify this: before I had Marcus, I only thought I had control over my life. As I soon learned, children have a way of laughing at this belief, just before they flush it down the toilet.

In the years prior to motherhood, I tried to make good decisions about my life. Of course, I made plenty of stupid choices along the way, but life had a way of letting me know I was being a dolt, so I was able to make corrections. This gave me the impression that I was in charge of things.

When I found out I was pregnant, I had a plan. It involved taking maternity leave a little early so I could decorate the baby's room and shop for diapers. I was also going to continue to take walks and get light exercise, to make it easier to get my pre-baby body back.

About two months from my due date, I was diagnosed with pre-eclampsia and had to be on bed rest. Although my maternity leave started early, there was no walking, no shopping, and no decorating. They had been replaced with lying around watching talk shows, and visiting the doctor for weekly amniocentesis.

Suddenly, Plan One had been scrapped before it had even been tried.

Two months later, when Dale and I took our baby boy home, I planned to be a good mom. I would rock him to sleep, I would nap when he napped, I would nurture this child in every way possible.

This would have worked if Marcus hadn't made plans of his own.

First of all, he didn't want to be rocked. He wanted us to walk him. Every night, Dale or I would roam the hallway between the bedrooms, trying to get him to sleep. He wasn't a difficult baby, he was just a wakeful one. I didn't nap when he napped because he didn't sleep very much. Instead, he was awake and expecting to be fed and entertained. I wasn't a mom; I was dinner and a show.

Feeding him was easy until he started on solid foods and decided he didn't like anything on the menu. I thought I'd feed him healthy meals, but I got to the point where I'd have fed him M&Ms and a Diet Coke if he'd eaten it.

And that pre-pregnancy body? Let's not go there. It's too depressing.

As I watched each of my plans being dismantled, I started to question whether I ever had control over anything. I had a nice career, but it had been up to my employer to hire me. My condo was nice, but I was fortunate to have good neighbors. I was in good physical shape, but my family history does include heart disease and diabetes.

For a while, I still believed I was in charge of my own thoughts, but that was abandoned when a driver cut me off in traffic one day and I thought of what I'd like to do to him if it was legal.

So, having a baby taught me all about control, and I'm still learning. Now that I'm the mother of a teenager, it's a wonder I have control over any of my faculties.

LET THE ADULTING BEGIN

Marcus is a senior this year at Valencia High School, a fact that fills me with equal parts pride and fear. The good news is, he has a high grade point average and a plan for college. The bad news is, he is a teenager. I try to focus on his level-headedness, but I keep worrying about his underage brain cells.

He was recently accepted to both the All State Honor Choir and the All State Jazz Choir. These events will take place in San Jose and Sacramento, respectively, on back-to-back weekends in March. Dale and I are both very proud, even though our bank account is whining.

Back in November, I tried to discourage Marcus from auditioning for both choirs. I pointed out the cost of two weekends in northern California. He pointed out the advantages of working with two directors that could help him with a career in music. I reminded him of school obligations he might have during March. He verified that there were no major tests or performances during that time.

I'm glad he's not a bad seed, because I can't out-debate him.

I used my last line of defense. "Go ahead and audition," I said. "We'll leave it up to God."

I thought the Almighty would look at our bank account, but all I heard was laughter coming from Heaven.

"I'm jealous," one of my friends told me. "Marcus is such a good kid." She has two adorable children who are bright, precocious, and skilled at pushing their parents' buttons.

"Don't be," I replied. "He's seventeen. There's still time for him to throw it all away."

She was skeptical, but I meant it. No matter how smart and focused and reasonable your child is, I believe they are capable of the same mindlessness that causes rabbits to suddenly leap into the road, under your tires.

As a matter of fact, this was one of my primary fears when Marcus got his driver's permit. I wasn't concerned about him driving recklessly. I was more worried that he'd drive very cautiously, then have a "random rabbit" moment and run up over the sidewalk for no reason.

Just last weekend, I had an example of this. We spent three days at a cabin in Idyllwild with friends. Dale had to leave early on Sunday to get some work done, so Marcus stepped up, unasked, to help me load the van. He carried suitcases, bags, even the cooler, and then emptied the trash. He even kept tabs on the football game Dale was missing, and texted the latest score to him. I was so proud of my grownup son. The only thing left to do was check out and get Mikey, the dog, into the car.

"I'm going to stop by the other cabin, then check out at the office," I said. "Mikey's with you."

As I walked toward our friends' cabin, I heard footsteps behind me. It was Marcus, alone.

"Where are you going?" I asked. "And where's Mikey?"

"In the cabin. Where are you going?"

My frustration showed. "What did I tell you I was going to do?"

"Honestly, Mom, I wasn't paying a bit of attention."

The vision of my son as an adult dissolved into a picture of a university student, happily enjoying college life, while oblivious to the term papers and other projects that are due.

I'm trying to let Marcus make his own decisions and accept his own consequences, but I wonder how old he'll be before I stop fretting over his ability to choose wisely. I know it will age me significantly.

ADVANCING TOWARD OLD AGE

They say age is "just a number." They also call it "a state of mind." I'm having another birthday in a few weeks, and I think the numbers are messing with the state of my mind.

It's bad enough that I look in the mirror and wonder why my outsides look older than I feel on the inside. My inner self thinks I'm still that woman in her 30's, who can do a handstand flip in her old dance group, and who can shop at The Limited because she fits their demographic. Unfortunately, the woman in the mirror cannot do justice to the styles in the young, hip stores, and the last time my heels were over my head, I had just fallen off my horse.

In addition to the external changes, I've been blessed with my own private summers. A doctor on the Internet reported that some women have twenty hot flashes a week. I was having twenty a day before I broke down and saw my doctor, Jerald Thanos, who gave me a lovely prescription to keep me from bursting into flames on an hourly basis.

Recently, I've noticed another disturbing trend, one I'm blaming on my advancing age; I want practical gifts. In my youth, I wanted clothes, jewelry, and frivolous things. As a matter of fact, my frivolity earned me a Barbie doll collection. Several years ago, I saw Enchanted Evening Barbie at Toys R Us. Her hair and makeup were very retro, and reminded me of my own Barbie back in the 60's. In some kind of wild-haired moment, I put her on my Christmas list.

Since then, I've gotten a Barbie doll every Christmas. Mostly, they're of the high-end, limited-edition kind. One year I got April in Paris Barbie. I asked if I'd find two tickets to France in her tiny suede purse. Dale just laughed.

"I thought of it, but, no," he said.

Nowadays, I don't ask for Barbies, or jewelry, or anything frivolous. I have a hard enough time shopping for my clothes, since I don't know how to dress my age. I'm hovering in jeans and t-shirts until I figure it out. If I can't get new clothes, I don't need to try to match jewelry to them. And Barbie reminds me that she is perennially young, while I am, hmm, not.

This year for my birthday, I want something I can use. I want a new mailbox.

Our mailbox is a small, wooden affair with a hinged door and shingles on its little roof. Sadly, the Santa Ana winds have removed a good portion of the shingles, and rust has removed the hinge and the door. The door removal was aided by the time a wasp built its nest inside, a fact we discovered it when the critter flew out and stung the mailman. I've already received soggy mail due to the rain seepage, so I'd like a nice, new box to magically appear on the post, with a red bow.

I'd also like a new alarm clock. This seems almost frivolous, since our current alarm clock works, in theory. It's one of those clocks that projects the time on the ceiling. The problem is the display on the face no longer lights up, so if the room's not dark enough, I can't read the time on the clock. I suppose if the room's not dark anymore, I should just get out of bed, but that's beside the point.

Considering the alternative, I'd like to recommend this aging process, but my heart's not in it. At the rate I'm going, pretty soon I'll be shopping for comfortable shoes.

READ ALL ABOUT IT

I'm happy to report that Dale reads my columns. Although I didn't get a new mailbox for my birthday, I did get a new alarm clock. It's a really nice one, with two alarms and a docking station for my iPod.

Unlike the men in my house, one of the joys of owning new equipment, for me, is to read the instructions. Digging the user's manual out of a crisp new box is like discovering some ancient manuscript. Will it answer all of life's mysteries? If not, will it at least tell me how to assemble everything?

After I've picked through the diagrams and understand how to make the gadget work, my next step is to read all of the warnings. This isn't because I want to know what not to do, it's because I can't believe they have to tell people not to put their toasters in the bathtub.

One evening I was looking at the warnings on my new curling iron. "Do not use while sleeping," it said. How can you sleep with a curling iron? It's meant to be a quick way to curl your hair. Wrap a strand, count to five, then unwrap. A five second nap would hardly be restful.

"I can't believe this warning," I told Dale.

"You know someone's tried it," he said.

So I suppose someone has washed their alarm clock in the dishwasher, hung it on the wall with duct tape, covered all the air vents, stored it in the microwave, and used it to hang wet laundry. At least, I think that's why those are all included in the list of what not to do.

My new alarm is so concerned about safety, the manual lists the same warnings in multiple places. On the first two pages, I am told four times not to get the alarm wet. First, I am warned about "rain and moisture", clearly an indication that these are two different types of wetness. Next, I am given a warning to keep it away from water in general. Finally, I have two statements about splashing, dripping, or other liquids. One statement is for the "apparatus", and the other is for the "appliance."

Since the radio came in one piece, I'm not sure which warning I should heed.

By contrast, I'm pretty sure my two guys have never read so much as a phrase that started out, "Insert tab A into slot B". Dale has the innate, masculine ability to open a box, take out the pieces and put it all together without looking at a piece of paper. Of course, I'm not sure all the pieces get used, but the thing works so I can't complain.

As for Marcus, from the time he was old enough for his own early-learning computer games, he automatically tossed anything aside that looked like directions, preferring to load the disk in the computer and find his way around the screen.

Unfortunately, even though they won't read the directions, they also won't throw them out. This summer I cleaned our spare bedroom, where we keep our file cabinet with important documents. Part of my task involved sifting through piles of papers and deciding what to keep, what to toss, and what to shred. By the end of my chore I had a stack of instruction manuals, all in their original packaging, untouched by human hands. I tried to save the ones for gadgets we still owned, but I won't swear that I succeeded.

No matter what, I am keeping the manual for my new clock. It's a real page turner.

YOU SAY EXCUSE, I SAY JUSTIFICATION

A long time ago, when I was a young software engineer, I had to report the status of my part of a project to some very big dogs in the department. It was stressful, because the project in general was behind in every way, which meant that I was behind in my tasks. This is not something you want to admit to the big dogs, unless you like being treated like kibble.

I went to my boss with my report, sweating anxiety, but he was nonplussed.

"If the rest of the project was on schedule, where would you be?"

After some quick calculations, I said, "A week ahead."

He smiled. "There's your status. You're a week ahead on the tasks you've planned, given the current project state."

I learned a very important lesson that day: it's not the number of beans you have, it's the way you count them that matters.

This little theory served me well in my job. Every project was measured against the reality of where we were, as opposed to the fantasy of where we'd told everyone we'd be. I guess that's how the big dogs of business work.

I've tried to apply this theory to my household tasks, but it's not as successful. The laundry isn't truly finished until it's out of the dryer and folded (put away is extra credit). Marking my task as 100% complete because I only planned to sort the lights and darks is useless when I'm out of socks.

What does work for me at home is the theory of Cost Per Use. If I know I'm going to use or wear an item a lot, I can justify a little higher cost if it's going to last longer. For example, I wear jeans at the ranch every day, even in the summer, so I buy jeans that are well constructed of durable material. By the time they're full of holes, I've probably spent a dime or less per wear.

My laptop recently died. It spent an entire day ignoring its AC outlet and telling me the battery was dead. Even though it was 4 years old, I have an extended warranty, so I was able to send it to a shop to be repaired or replaced. The bad news is that it takes a minimum of ten days to do this, which basically cripples me.

So I considered my options. Marcus has a laptop. I could download the files I needed on his computer, and use it for 10 days. Our only problem would be scheduling. It's easy to think I'd use it in the daytime and he'd use it in the evening, but sometimes my days are filled with activities and I have to do my writing in the evenings. There would be arm-wrestling sooner or later.

My second option was to purchase a new laptop. I could get a new model for half the price, so I did the math. My old laptop's cost per use was less than a dollar a day. If a new laptop lasts 4 years, it would cost less than 50 cents a day.

At the end of the day, I bought a new Dell. It's got a bazillion Gigabytes of everything and is so fast it travels through time. At least, that's what it feels like, which is why I should never write ad copy.

But I think I counted my beans just right. Of course, I'll have two laptops after the old one is repaired. But what's wrong with having a backup?

THE BALLS AREN'T JUGGLING THEMSELVES

As the school year winds down, activities ramp up. There are multiple concerts, end of the year banquets, awards nights and more. For the past few weeks, every night has been filled with something to do. When we're not in the auditorium listening to music, Dale and I are in the old gymnasium, making decorations for Grad Night.

It would all be so much easier if normal life could be put on hold, but bills need to be paid, groceries need to be purchased, and the house needs to stay semi-organized. I'd like to push the 'pause' button on these things, if I could only find the remote control.

In the quietest times of life, my house hovers on the brink of clutter-mania, but when no one has time to put anything back where it belongs, we end up with Clutter-Palooza. Important receipts I've printed are stacking up beside the printer. The gift basket Dale won at the band concert is sitting in the dining room. Even Dale and Marcus' Easter goodies are still on the kitchen table.

Although there are things in every room that belong in a different place, the family room bears the brunt of our disarray. In addition to five pairs of Dale's shoes, and whatever Marcus has brought home from school, I have stacks of paper on the fireplace, all revolving around choir or graduation.

At some point, I don't know whether to try to clean the house or just hire a bulldozer.

The mail tends to come in and rest in clumps on various flat surfaces, where it gets rearranged by the cat. I try to pull out the important-looking envelopes, but even they just get moved to their own bundle. Fortunately, most of my bills are paperless, but there are a few companies that haven't gotten on the green bandwagon, so I know I need to be watching for the statement from the horse shoer, or the medical lab.

I've become a sort of money psychic during this madness. Every few days, I wake with an elevated heart rate and sudden shortness of breath, thinking, "I forgot to pay the such-and-such bill." I then rush to the computer and schedule the payment.

I don't recommend this system, even though I do count it as aerobic exercise.

As for buying food, I don't even remember the last time I went grocery shopping with a full list that included dinners for the week. I've made little trips for milk and cereal for Marcus. I've been able to keep Dale in snack foods to eat while he watches the basketball playoffs. On a few, rare nights, I've run to the store for some meat and vegetables to fix dinner because we're all home together. Otherwise, it's been a cornucopia of fast food, I'm sorry to say.

You know you're eating out too much when the girl at the counter of Carl's Jr. asks, "Will you be having the usual?"

During the day, I feel like a deer in the woods, foraging for food. Breakfast and lunch consist of whatever I can dig out of the pantry. So far, this has included canned green beans, chicken noodle soup, and lots of peanut butter on crackers.

The other day, I found a can of tuna and thought I'd hit the jackpot. Unfortunately, so did the Katy the cat, who was also out of food.

Good thing I like peanut butter.

The whirlwind will end in soon, but I'm getting so used to the chaos, I'm starting to wonder: will normal life be too boring now?

ADVICE FOR A GOOD LIFE

I like to read the inspirational speeches made by famous people at graduation ceremonies. I often think, *gee, I'd like to make a speech at a graduation some day.* Then I remember, they only ask inspirational people to make those speeches.

I'm pretty sure I don't qualify.

As a horsewoman, my first piece of advice would be to tell the graduates never to squat on their spurs. When it comes to horses, my inexperience has resulted in being stepped on, jumped on, bitten, kicked, and picking myself off the dirt while my horse wonders why I'm not in the saddle. There's not much inspiration there.

The rest of my life isn't that much better. I started out well enough. My early years were spent getting straight A's, doing what my parents said, and being a good little girl. In the meantime, my brother was getting B's because, "it was easy" and being the class (and family) clown.

With that kind of history, I'm not sure how I became the humor writer.

Nevertheless, if I could talk to the graduates, this is what I would tell them:

So far, you've spent your whole life focused on school. You've read text books and listened to lectures. You've written papers. You've taken tests. You're now about to be handed a piece of paper that says you're ready to step into the next round. Whether the next round involves getting a job or getting more education, I have an important message for you.

You haven't really been prepared.

If you're moving from high school to college, it may be more years of text books and tests, but it's not quite the same. For one thing, your mom cannot come to your dorm room every morning and wake you up for class. For another, your professors do not care if you attend class. They don't care if you turn in your assignments. They don't even care if you flunk out. The only people who care are the ones who are paying for your education.

Forget the bank—Mom and Dad may impose severe penalties for your early withdrawal.

If you're moving into a career, I have some good news and some bad news. The good news is, you'll never have to remember who fought the War of 1812. And, unless you've chosen a career as a rocket scientist, you'll never have to solve for X again. Your boss won't care.

The bad news is, your boss won't care about a lot of things you did really well in school. Surviving school involves completing a lot of short-term assignments, taking tests and above all, keeping your eyes on your own paper. The workplace is, well, different. Assignments are usually long-term projects, so you have to figure out how to meet a lot of little deadlines in order to complete the whole task. You'll have other team members who have to meet their deadlines, too, and if someone drops the ball, everyone will share the blame. This is called "working well with others."

Too bad they don't teach classes in how to survive the workplace.

There is more good news, in a way. In school, you frequently get one chance at a grade. If you fail a test, you don't get to re-take it. At work, if you mess something up, you get to do it over until either it's fixed or you're fired, which isn't such good news after all.

Maybe I should have stuck with the advice about the spurs.

WHO'S BEING TRAINED HERE?

Now that Marcus is safely installed at Cal State Long Beach, people have been asking how I'm adjusting to my empty nest. I don't know what they're talking about.

I have a puppy.

Duffy is almost six months old now. He's sweet and playful. He's also stubborn, and willful, beyond any puppy I've ever raised. When I put his first collar on him, he rolled around the kitchen as if he was having a seizure. He did this, uninterrupted, for over an hour before he got tired. Then he went to his crate and pouted. Dale was amazed, and told everyone about our pouting dog.

"Dogs don't pout," someone said.

"You've never seen this dog," my husband told them. "He just lays there. Won't eat. Won't play. Won't come out of his crate."

It took Duffy two weeks to accept his collar as status quo. Until then, I had a dog who rolled, pouted, rolled, pouted, etc., all day. I was exhausted from watching him.

He's getting better about learning to be a good dog. Potty training is high on the list, followed by coming when called, and leaving shoes, papers and electrical wires alone.

It's hard not to compare him with Mikey, since they are the same breed. Dale seems to think Duffy is not as smart, but I disagree. In many ways, he's smarter than our late companion.

For example, he has already trained us that he will not fetch the clean toy we throw for him, but only the slobbery one he has been chewing on. If we try to throw the clean toy, he sits and barks at us until we pick up the wet one and toss it.

As far as potty training, after he wets the floor, he whines at us to come clean it up. I am currently in negotiations with him to reverse this activity and whine first so I can open the door and let him out. All I can say is, we may need to call in an arbiter.

Coming when called is a hit or miss exercise. If he is not doing something important, like running across the lawn with my shoe, he will come. Otherwise, he will acknowledge that he's been called, by pausing to look at me, and then run the opposite direction.

Lately, he's been engaging in Michigan J. Frog activities. There was an old cartoon about a frog that sang and danced, but only for the man who discovered him. The poor sap went broke trying to exploit his little green gold mine, and finally put him back where he found him when he couldn't.

When Duffy and I are home alone, I can tell him to get his toy, and he returns with his plush toy for playing tug. I can also tell him to get his ball, and he finds his tennis ball to play fetch. When Dale comes home and I try to repeat these acts, Duffy sits at my feet with a quizzical look.

"I don't think he's very smart," Dale says.

"No, really, he knows the words." I try again. "Duffy, get your toy."

The dog looks at me like I'm crazy. So does my husband.

This week, we're trying a new potty training tactic. A woman told me to hang a bell on the back door.

"The dog will associate the sound of the bell with going out to potty," she said. "He'll start ringing it to go out."

Maybe he will. Or maybe he'll just learn to ring the bell for maid service.

AH! AT LAST, ADVICE I CAN SHARE

A friend of mine announced her pregnancy the other day. It's her first baby, and everyone is excited. Even though she's young, she qualifies as an Older Mom according to the doctors.

I was also the Older Mom when I had Marcus, so I thought I could give her some good advice. The first thing I told her was that she'd be now getting a flood of suggestions, and most of them would contradict each other, including mine.

Suddenly, I thought I might not have anything useful to offer.

I'm sure there have been changes in the way the medical community handles pregnancies in general, and Older Moms in particular. For example, when I was pregnant, I was told that eating fish was good for me. Alcohol was forbidden. Weight gain was limited to twenty-five pounds. Mild exercise was recommended.

Now I hear fish is off the menu, a glass of champagne on New Year's is allowed, and as for exercise, keep doing what you've always done, just don't start anything new.

One good piece of advice is to listen to the doctor. That never changes.

As I recall, I tried to be an obedient patient. I just didn't always communicate well with my doctor. When he told me I was on bed rest due to my high blood pressure, I thought that meant just general resting. I can do a load of laundry while I'm lying around, right?

He put me in the hospital for a week to teach me what the term "bed rest" meant.

Our miscommunications continued when I went in for a C-section. The epidural wasn't quite strong enough. I was trying to ask if I should feel anything. He was trying to find out what I felt. The anesthetist ended up giving me a triple dose of whatever they were serving. They could have sawed me in half at that point.

Another good piece of advice is to be flexible. I thought I'd be mobile until the baby was due. I had plans to decorate the room, shop for baby things, get some exercise.

Those plans didn't include pre-eclampsia, but that's what happened, and I lounged around for the last two months instead. Every evening Dale came home to a new list of what I thought we needed for the baby, along with a new food craving for dinner. I admit, I was a little sad whenever I thought about my abandoned intentions.

I could also tell her to go ahead and acknowledge her feelings. Pregnancy comes with some sadness and lots of fear. Changes are coming, and they may not be the good kind, like when you get a new appliance. Babies don't come with an instruction manual.

The first day I was left alone with Marcus, I spent the whole day telling myself to just get through this minute, then this one, then this one. People assume the Older Mom doesn't need any help, as if maturity is some kind of magic that turns you into a parent. What if he's crying and I can't stop him? What if it's serious? What if I don't recognize it's serious?

In the end, he survived my parenting with no ill effects.

I was born in the 50's, where I'm pretty sure doctors' advice was to limit martinis to two a day and the cigarettes to half a pack. My mom drank coffee by the pot and never had a meal without something fried on the plate. I turned out fine.

Perhaps the best advice is to accept you're doing your best. In the end, it will be what it will be.

PLAYING POSSUM

Pets, like children, are not for the faint of heart, nor the weak of stomach. I've always thought that anyone who isn't sure about having a child should start with a cat. Not only will they ignore you almost as much as a teenager, if you can't clean up a hairball without gagging, maybe parenthood isn't for you.

Dogs can be messier than cats, or even some teenagers. The world is their toy box. Everything exists for them to dig up, chew, rip apart, and then abandon in search of the next target.

Duffy discovered the wonders of the backyard as a puppy. Unfortunately, he likes to bring his toys into the house to play. It started with sections of the sugar cane Dale is growing in one corner of the yard. Sugar cane is rather bamboo-like in structure, so I had shredded vegetation all over the kitchen floor every day for a month or so.

Once I deterred him from the cane, he found large sticks. These could also be chewed into pieces. Now that his world had opened to include the kitchen and the family room, I was picking wooden shrapnel off the carpet.

I got that stopped, when the Santa Ana winds deposited new toys in the yard, including a small clay pot and a dirt clod. I was actually okay with the flower pot, but I was too slow to stop the clod from becoming dust. One swift bite with puppy teeth scattered it across the rug.

At least the vacuum picks up dirt easier than kindling.

But sticks, dirt, and random garden equipment are mere trinkets when I compare them with what he brought in this week.

It was a little past eight in the morning. Duffy ran to his pillow by the window with something in his mouth, which he began to tear apart. Not wanting to pick up more debris, I ordered him to drop it. It looked like a gnarled plant root of some kind, so I picked it up and turned it over. That's when I saw what it really was.

A row of sharp teeth smiled up at me from the bleached side, petrified whiskers lying flat against the ridge of where a nose used to be, a divot where there once was an eye—a beady little eye. I was holding a possum skull, in my bare hand.

The horror was immediate. I could hear the screeching violins of "Psycho" pulsing in my head, and the room suddenly went black-and-white, like an old movie. I wanted to drop the object and scream like a girl, but I knew Duffy would grab it and run.

As much as I hated holding that thing, I didn't want to be cleaning it out of my vacuum.

I tried to run to the trash to throw it away, although my feet didn't move nearly as fast as my brain ordered them. It's possible that I was saying, "Eew-eew-eew," the entire way.

The rest of the day was spent quietly, with Duffy asleep in the recliner while I washed my hands every ten minutes. After a few hours, I had removed two or three layers of skin and felt better.

The biggest surprise was when Dale got home and I told him what happened.

"Where could he have found a possum skull?" I asked.

Dale looked at me, sheepish. "I found it. I guess I left it by the pool."

"Why?"

"Because it looked cool."

Perhaps it's better to move from kids to pets instead. Marcus never made me pick up vermin bones.

A TIRING EXCURSION

On a scale of bad to horrific, I think having an accident on the freeway leans toward the latter. Not only is your car injured, you might be hurt, and you can hit other cars if you spin out of control. Add my fear of having to sit so close to the steering wheel that the air bag will snap my neck like a twig if it ever inflates, and you know why I'm such a careful driver on the freeways.

Being careful isn't always enough, as I learned last weekend.

I had just finished attending the Placentia Library Friends Foundation's Author's Luncheon, where John Dean revealed a lot of things I never knew about Watergate. It was still early, so I thought I'd scamper up to a library in Ontario to listen to a friend of mine speak about being a mystery writer.

That may sound crazy, but when you're a writer, you can't get enough of libraries and other writers.

Traffic was unusually heavy for a Saturday afternoon. I found myself on the 60 freeway, shooting along like a rocket in a sea of missiles, all at 70 miles per hour. There was no way to go slower, or to get out of the herd, until I reached my exit. By the way, the 60 freeway is in no condition to drive 70 miles per hour. I'm pretty certain there are roads in Afghanistan that are in better shape.

I was about two miles from my exit when I saw a clump of paper in my lane. There were cars on either side of me and it was just paper, so I went ahead and drove over it.

It turns out, the clump was not paper.

I'm still not sure what it was, but the sound underneath my car was a combination of a rasp scraping metal and a bullet ricocheting in a tin can. As a last act of mischief, the thing threw itself under my back tire.

There's probably an expert out there who'll tell me what I should have done at that point. What I did was to say a swear word, cross my fingers, and continue toward my goal.

I exited on Euclid and continued north, toward the library. About four blocks from my destination, I felt my car move a little sluggishly. Two blocks later, it was evident that my left back tire was flat.

Immediately, I thought I should pull over and call Triple-A. It would mean missing my friend's talk at the library, however, which was only two blocks away…

I slowed down and coasted into the library parking lot, while a man in a large, 80's style sedan drove beside me, honking all the way. He kept waving at me to tell me my tire was flat, and I kept waving at him to tell him I knew already.

It was a lovely exchange, and I hope we can keep in touch.

My friend was glad to see me and I had a wonderful time at the library. Afterward, a young man from Triple-A came out and exchanged my very flat tire for the donut stored underneath my car.

I was relieved the donut was uninjured in the attack.

At the end of the day, all I had left to do was drive home from Ontario to Placentia on surface streets. It only took me an hour to finally pull into my drive. On Monday, I limped my car to Allen, who fitted me with a new tire.

On a scale of bad to horrific, I'd rate this accident a *could-have-been-worse*.

DIRECTIONALLY CHALLENGED

As I've watched Marcus grow, I can see his similarities to Dale and me, both in physical looks and in behavior. He's got Dale's cheekbones and my smile, Dale's athletic ability and my sense of humor. I was hoping he'd have my organizational gene, but he inherited Dale's "leave it somewhere then hunt for it later" DNA.

Unfortunately, I've learned from his recent experiences with the car that he's got my sense of direction.

I used to think I always knew where I was, I just wasn't always where I wanted to be. But after listening to my son's tales of wandering down the wrong freeway, I must own my "getting lost" gene.

In my early days of living here, I sometimes spent half an hour trying to figure out which freeway I was on, before discovering it was the wrong one. I can read maps, which is helpful, but if there's a little zigzag in the road, I often zig when I should zag. Mapquest can confuse me because it gives too much information. Why is it important to tell me to drive a tenth of a mile on the off-ramp? Is there any other way for me to go?

I try to rely on the navigation app in my phone. Wanda the Wonder Navigator is useful for telling me which lane to be in for freeway entrances. She can be awfully mean-spirited, however. Twice now, she has directed me to the carpool-only entrance of the 5 freeway from Main Street in Santa Ana. It is not well marked, so the first time, I took it and spent a couple of miles in a panic because I didn't belong there and couldn't get out of the lane.

How was I going to explain that to Highway Patrol? "Wanda made me do it," would get me one ticket for the carpool violation and another one for being an idiot.

To be fair to my son, he can make his way around Placentia without a problem, and around Long Beach as well. It's just when he tries to connect the two, he runs into trouble. His first trip went well, except for missing the entrance to the 57 freeway from the 22, but he recognized Glassell, so he was able to get home.

The second time he went to Long Beach, I wasn't worried. When he arrived, he texted me to say he got there, but he accidentally got on the 91 and not on the 22. Instead of turning around and getting back to the 22, he just kept traveling on the 91 until he recognized a street that runs past his campus, Bellflower Boulevard.

Let's just say he saw a lot of neighborhoods before he got to Long Beach.

The third time, he got in the wrong lane and ended up on the 405-south. Instead of turning around and getting back to the 22, he kept driving on the 405 until he decided he didn't recognize any of these streets. Then he exited the freeway, pulled over in a parking lot, and called me. It turns out, he was in Westminster.

I guess I'm glad he wasn't in San Diego.

If you're seeing a pattern here, so am I. When I realize I am going the wrong direction, I find a way to turn around and get back on track. When my son realizes he's going the wrong direction, he keeps going until his course corrects itself.

Unless it doesn't. Then he calls me.

It's probably my fault. I should have included a "U-turn" gene with the "easily lost" one.

DON'T DO IT LIKE THIS

I do a lot of silly things. Some might even call them stupid. In order to use my talents for good instead of evil, I share my foibles in this column, in an attempt to keep others from repeating my mistakes.

Like the time I wrote about forgetting my wedding anniversary. I knew it was in May, but we had just moved into our new home and my head was still full of things like transferring utilities and changing our address. So I thought our anniversary was celebrated in the May that comes after June.

I know you won't make that mistake, now that you've heard about it from me.

Last Saturday, I had to teach riding lessons starting at nine a.m. Somehow, I managed to mess up the time and thought nine o'clock started at ten. I spent all morning scampering about, trying to recover from my error.

Take my advice and be certain when your appointments begin. Nine o'clock always starts at nine.

If you want to talk about horses, my general clumsiness around 1,000-pound pets is legendary. I used to say at least I'd never been kicked—until I got kicked. I had a spectacular horseshoe-shaped bruise, in a most private location.

Don't get too close to a horse when they're playing.

As silly as some of my mistakes have been, they don't come close to what I witnessed a few weeks ago.

I was driving down Placentia Avenue, having shopped at Sam's Club and heading toward Albertson's to get a few more things. The light at Placentia and Chapman was red, so I stopped behind the first car at the light. I looked over to my right and saw the Placentia Police Department had a DUI checkpoint on Chapman.

In theory, I feel a lot safer knowing the police are trying to keep drunk drivers off the street. In practice, I was glad I didn't have to go through the checkpoint, not because I had been drinking. I mean, Sam's Club doesn't offer free samples of everything. I was just in a hurry to get my shopping done.

Even though I could clearly see the checkpoint from my car, the driver in front of me wasn't paying attention. He turned right on the red light, then apparently had second thoughts, and attempted to make a U-turn. All he managed to do was block all eastbound traffic on Chapman while he sat sideways in both lanes.

Finally, the light turned green and he un-wedged himself, continuing down Placentia Avenue. It's entirely possible the driver wasn't worried about a DUI. He might have decided he didn't want to wait in line at the checkpoint if he didn't have to.

Too bad he also didn't notice the motorcycle policeman sitting beside me at the light.

The officer noticed him, however. I let the motorcycle zip past me, which he was happy to do, lights flashing. As I drove on to the store, I saw the car pulling over. In the end, the driver should've taken his chances with the checkpoint. It would have been a shorter wait than the personal attention he was about to receive.

I may not have been the person making the mistake, but I learned valuable lessons I can pass to others. Always be aware of your surroundings. There is a point of no return.

And once you've decided to disobey the law, do check your mirrors for the policeman who will catch you.

CHATTING UP MY HUSBAND

I think Dale and I have a good marriage. At least, we have one that runs smoothly, mostly because we treat each other as equal partners, we each have our own hobbies, and we each know our roles.

For example, I'm the one who talks.

Dale does speak, on occasion, but he prefers to save his words for important events, like watching sports on TV, or describing his experiences with coaching children's basketball teams. He leaves the silly blathering about nothing to me.

So his recent visit to Tampa, Florida surprised me, in terms of his general chattiness.

When he goes on a trip, he usually calls or texts to let me know he got to his location. I don't get much more than that, unless something truly remarkable happens to him, which is not often. Dale's basic philosophy is, if there's anything I need to know, the police will notify me.

That's the Dale I expected when he went to the NCAA Frozen Four hockey tournament with his friends, Brian and Tracy. Travel plans were to fly from Orange County to Tampa via Dallas. Unfortunately, they were traveling right after the tornadoes hit Texas. Dale left home at 5:30 that morning for John Wayne Airport.

At 7 a.m. I got my first text from him. "New travel plans, waiting for the shuttle to LAX. Flight to Atlanta leaves at 1:30."

By noon, I had three more texts detailing the stand-by flights they had tried, unsuccessfully, to get on. They were now leaving for Atlanta at 4:30. I responded as optimistically as I could, but sometimes there wasn't much to say after he told me about the last stand-by that had slipped through their fingers.

As they waited at LAX, he texted me that he was at the bar and had just given a napkin to the lead singer from Air Supply.

I had a response to that. "Does he still have his hair? And is he still all out of love?"

"Looks like his picture," he replied. "Brian found it on his iPhone. Who else will sit next to me that I don't know? I need someone from R&B."

Several texts later, he was on the plane to Atlanta, which would arrive around 9:30 p.m. Oddly, he never texted or called to say he made it to Tampa. I guess he was too tired by that time.

For the rest of the trip, however, he was very chatty with his texts, describing where they were and what they were doing. He even sent me a picture of the baseball stadium where they went to a Tampa Bay Rays game.

I was supposed to pick all three men up at John Wayne Airport on Sunday, so our phones were busy that day, coordinating when to expect them. Their 8:30 p.m. arrival was pushed back to 10:30. When I got there, the plane had landed, and Brian was by the curb, but Tracy and Dale had to wait for their bags at the carousel.

The security officer couldn't have been nicer, but insisted I could not wait there for them. As I was pulling away, Tracy came out. Brian stayed and waited for Dale while Tracy rode with me for one more trip around the lot. I suppose he was worried I might get lost.

Finally, all three men were in my minivan and I dropped them off at their homes. I was happy to have Dale back, although I don't know whether I actually missed him.

We talked more that weekend than we ever do.

WHEN DRAMA'S JUST DUCKY

Our pool is old. It's small and made of fiberglass, so there are not a lot of options to restore it. Some would say it's time to replace it, but Dale is not a man who gives up easily. In his world, anything can be fixed.

Perhaps we should send him to solve the Mideast problem.

Every weekend, he fusses with the pool, cleaning it, adjusting filters and trying anything that might restore it to its former glory. Recently, he bought a new motor and has made several trips to the pool store for pipes and screws and whatever you need to hook up a new motor to an old pool.

While he's doing all this, the water level is down about halfway, making it even less useable. I'm just trying to ignore it until he either fixes it or tells me how much it will cost to replace it.

In my world, ignorance is bliss.

This week, however, something happened to call my attention to the pool in a most dramatic way. I had just dressed for the day when I heard ducks quacking over the house. I assumed they were on their way to Tri-City Park, or some other location with plenty of water for swimming and dirt for insect hunting.

A few moments later, I heard splashing. It sounded like it was coming from our backyard, but I was certain no one would be in our pool. The splashing continued, growing more violent, so I went to the sliding glass door and opened the blinds.

What I saw was a death match, indeed happening in our little half-filled puddle. Two male mallards were fighting furiously, each one trying to pin the other one by the back of the neck so he could push his head under the water.

I certainly did not want a drowned duck in our pool. Yes, they're just ducks, but the scene would haunt me every time I went for a swim. Plus, it's unsanitary to have a dead duck anywhere, except your freezer. I thought about pounding on the glass and chasing them both away.

A brief vision crossed my mind, of crime scene tape, a police interrogation, and a tiny little stretcher hauling Daffy away in a black bag. The crime scene unit would dust for web-footed prints, and I'd have to work with a sketch artist to identify the killer.

Just as I opened the blinds to pound on the glass, one of the mallards decided he'd had quite enough, and flew away. The remaining duck appeared nonplussed, then began to dip himself repeatedly in the water, stretching up to flap his wings every so often.

That's when I saw the whole picture: a small female floated from her hiding spot in the corner and joined the male in the whole dipping, flapping ritual. I must say, she looked a little proud of herself, wiggling her tail feathers and eyeing the male.

After they completed their baths, the pair hopped out to the deck and stood in the sun, eyes closed, basking in the warmth. I was so amazed, I texted Dale with the story of the fight.

"In our half-filled pool?" was his response. "They're usually at the neighbor's."

I thought about my little murder scene and changed it to a black-and-white noir movie, with Humphrey Bogart.

"It's always about some dame, isn't it?" he'd ask the detective.

Perhaps Dale is right and the pool is still useful. After all, it supplied me with a lot of entertainment that morning, and maybe even a scene in my next book.

WORKING FOR A TOUGH BOSS

The media keeps telling us the economy is improving. The stock market is holding steady, more or less. Unemployment is down, in some places. Unfortunately, all this good news has not paid off for our son.

It has now been a month since Marcus finished his first year of college, three months since he started applying for jobs in the area, and he is still unemployed. In recent weeks, he has spent entire days applying for jobs, from restaurants to retail stores. He's learning a lot about filling out forms and talking to managers.

It's a skill he'd like to trade for an actual paycheck.

His biggest problem is his availability. It would be easier if he could promise part time hours when he goes back to school, but working near our home and living in the Long Beach dorms doesn't seem feasible.

As I watched him struggle these past weeks, I thought, maybe I could pay him to help me around the house. Then I thought, no, maybe he needs to find a real job.

Dale was also thinking about Marcus' problem.

"We should hire him," he told me. "We could pay him a couple hundred bucks to work around the house, run errands. He could even drive my mother to the grocery store."

"A couple hundred bucks? A week?"

I wasn't thinking about paying our son that much, but I mulled it over. If I gave him a minimum number of hours, I could be comfortable with the arrangement. I put together a list of chores and a sheet to keep track of his time and presented him with the idea.

He didn't exactly leap for joy at our offer. I suspect verbs like "mop", "sweep" and "wash" might have deterred him. He read the list, which included everything from vacuuming to weeding the flower beds.

"How do I know when any of these needs doing?" he asked.

I swept my hand outward, in a very Vanna White moment. "Look around, Dear. It always needs doing."

After showing him the proper and scientifically proven way to clean, including washing dishes, I turned him loose. He considered my guidelines, and then did things his way. I did what any woman would do who has to live with her employee.

I closed my eyes and chanted "at least it's getting done."

His first week was a little rough on me. Chores tended to be completed between the hours of 6 and 9 p.m. Garden tools didn't always leave the garden and the only reason the broom was removed from the kitchen was to keep Duffy from tearing it apart. Toward the end of the week, he miscalculated and had to spend nine hours on Sunday finishing his minimum.

The first time I handed him the grocery list, however, I knew I would regret it when he went back to school. He even came home with the correct brand of everything.

We haven't sent him to take his grandmother grocery shopping yet. She lives in Norwalk and doesn't drive. My mother-in-law amazes me. She can get anywhere in the Los Angeles area using the bus system. She also raised four boys, all a year apart in age. I hope this gives her some patience with her grandson.

She's going to need steady nerves and clear directions to keep him from getting lost.

I suspect he's still on the lookout for that outside job, but in the meantime, I'm getting my windows washed and Dale and I feel like responsible citizens. We're doing our part to keep the unemployment rate down.

THERE'S NO CURE FOR THIS

It's been said that, like fine wine, people get better with age. If that's true, I think I may be a little musty and full of vinegar.

Like many people, I often feel younger than I actually am. It's always a shock to be talking to someone and catch my reflection in the mirror. I sound so much younger than that woman staring back at me.

I knew gravity worked. I just didn't know it worked on skin, too. And I always said I wouldn't mind having laugh lines, but do they have to extend across my face and down my neck? I must have laughed like an idiot in my youth.

Coming to terms with my ever-changing image might account for my increasing crankiness, along with the general aches of a body that doesn't bounce back the way it used to. I never knew I could sprain a rib just by tying my shoes.

The worst part of aging, however, is contracting But-First Disease. It's an incurable illness, where a person makes plans to do one thing, then thinks, "But first, I'll take care of this other thing."

And so goes the day. We don't get our important chores done because all the But-First tasks eat up the hours. It would be nice if my But-First tasks were as necessary as the ones I needed to do, but usually they could wait.

Last Wednesday, I needed to load my minivan with the setup for my booth at the Concerts in the Park. This included a portable canopy, a table, boxes of books, and my box of accessories—tablecloths, pens, book stands, and my two gnomes, Booker and Hatch (they are characters from the first book).

Fortunately, I hired my son to schlep everything into the van. Unfortunately, my accessory box had become a little disorganized after the book launch party, so I had to put everything back into it before Marcus could load it into the car.

But first…

I walked through my bedroom and glanced at the hamper. Had I washed the outfit I planned to wear? I needed to dig out my clothes and start a load of laundry. But first…

Katy the cat curled around my legs, meowing. Had she been fed? I looked into her room and saw she needed to have her dish washed out and new canned food opened, so I picked up her bowl. But first…

I passed by the dryer and saw a stack of unopened mail. Had I paid the car insurance? With Katy's bowl in my hand and Katy on my heels, I walked toward the family room to check the bank account on my laptop. But first…

The afternoon went like that until I finally stopped taking care of all my extraneous chores and made a beeline for the spare bedroom. It only took fifteen minutes to rearrange the box and get everything where it belonged, after which I gave Marcus the okay to load it up.

On Thursday, he helped me get everything to Tri-City Park, where I again fought against my But-First tendencies to set up the booth and books. In the end, it took forty-five minutes to perform a ten-minute task, but at least I was ready before the concert started.

The music was lots of fun and I met the most delightful readers, some of whom even bought my books. The event made me feel young again. Good thing there were no mirrors to tell me anything different.

As Bette Davis once said, old age ain't no place for sissies.

MOTHERHOOD'S MANY MOODS

My friend had her baby last week. She had announced her pregnancy around Christmas and I spent the last seven months re-visiting my own pregnancy with her, telling her it was normal when she could no longer tie her shoes, or even see her feet.

What I couldn't tell her was how it would feel to finally meet the stranger who had shared a most intimate space with her for nine months. Like her, I knew I was having a boy, had named him, talked about him and to him, but until I looked into his face, I had no idea how I'd feel about him.

For me, the Hallmark commercials got it wrong. I didn't get any gooey, sentimental feelings, like they use to describe a mother's love. Instead, I felt fierce, like a wild animal protecting her young. I used to think of myself as a Tiger Mom, but that means something different these days.

I guess you could call me a Really Mean Tabby Cat Mom.

Visiting my friend and her baby in the hospital brought back all those memories of my own son. Marcus may be a young man of eighteen now, but I still have a distinct muscle memory of holding him as an infant. He liked to be held chest to chest, and that impression of his little swaddled form in my arms remains with me.

Now he looms over me, looking down and draping his arms across my shoulders. When did he get so big?

I started thinking about his childhood. Certain ages came to mind, like snapshots in an album, along with his interests at the time.

He loved insects so we went to bug workshops at the zoo and night hikes in the nature center. We went through the same experience when he discovered reptiles.

I'd like to now confess, I don't like spiders and snakes. But when the cub wants to investigate new worlds, what's a Tabby Mom to do?

I told some of these stories to my friend, suggesting her little boy might like similar things.

"Ew, bugs," she said. "Not a big fan. Daddy may have to do the bugs."

"A great bonding experience for them," I agreed.

"Also not a big fan of snakes," she added.

"Maybe he won't like reptiles. But it could be more Dad time."

For Marcus, the reptile passion waned, as did the insects. These fascinations were traded for cars, dinosaurs, the Titanic, and Abraham Lincoln, among other things. Each time he approached a door of knowledge, Dale and I opened it for him.

When he discovered music, he began opening his own doors. The day he turned down the chance to do an easy Valtech internship at Raytheon in order to forge a new kind of technical internship at a recording studio, I knew he was in control of his interests. The Tabby Mom may be retired, but it's a joyful experience to watch my child pursue something he loves.

I'm certain my friend and her husband have no idea what their baby's interests will be. He might like pet rats and action figures. He may find his passion right away, or it may take him years of trying this and that to figure out what he wants to be when he grows up.

As far as that goes, I'm only guessing that Marcus will continue his musical path into a career. At the eleventh hour, he could chuck it all and become an engineer. Or a mechanic.

After all, what does a Really Mean Tabby Mom know about the future?

CLEANING FOR COMPANY

Our house has become more than quiet since Marcus went back to school. Not that he is a particularly rowdy son, but there's an energy missing from our home. Even Duffy whines that he's bored.

So I was very excited when a twenty-something year old friend from Sacramento asked if she and her girlfriend could spend a weekend at our house. It's true, they were only in town to spend as much time at Disneyland as possible, but they would liven things up while they were here.

Plus, it gave me an excuse to clean the house.

I'm hoping that I am not the only person with two types of housecleaning: one for family and one for company. I would like to have the extra-clean house all the time, but Dale and Marcus aren't so picky. This means either I have to do it all or I have to nag them to help me.

Either way, it's exhausting.

When it comes to my family, I can do the dishes and wipe the counters on a regular basis, but running a cloth across the furniture and vacuuming the carpet can be done semi-regularly. Suitcases don't have to be put away, extension cords can be left out on the bed in the spare room, and boxes of books can be stacked in any unused space, as long as the door is closed.

Those rooms can't stay that way if people are expected to sleep in them.

For three days, I put things in their appropriate places. I moved my books to the garage. Suitcases were stuffed back into the closet. I even stripped the spare beds and washed all the linens. I usually do this after every houseguest, but I couldn't remember the last time anyone visited.

All mail was separated into piles of Keep, Toss, and I Need to Keep It But I Don't Know Where to Put It. For the family, I would have set the leftover papers in two neater piles in the family room and filed them away, eventually. For guests, I needed to make them invisible, so I did what any other clean freak would do.

I put them in a box in the garage.

Floors were mopped. Carpets were vacuumed. Every counter was scrubbed. I even cleaned the top of the refrigerator and I'm pretty sure my guests weren't tall enough to see it.

By the time I was finished, the house was my kind of clean. It's impossible to maintain, but it makes me do a little happy dance.

Sara and April arrived Friday night and I showed them where to find their rooms, the bathroom, and the coffee. They were delightful houseguests and I enjoyed our mornings together before they took off for another marathon day at the Magic Kingdom.

Having spent so many years in a house full of men, it was fun to see two young girls get ready for the day. Between the hair products and the makeup and the clothing selections, it took at least two hours for them to prepare. At one point, I suggested maybe they should get up at five instead of six if they wanted to be at Disneyland by eight.

Sara said she actually considered it, but voted for sleep.

Three short days later, they were gone, along with their curling irons and girlish laughter. The house is quiet again, and Duffy is bored. I wouldn't mind having them around all the time, but if they moved in, would I be cleaning for family or for company?

Maybe I could just enjoy the energy and worry about dusting later.

THEY'RE ALWAYS YOUR KIDS

I remember how excited I was when our son, Marcus, took his first steps. I thought it would be nice to not have to carry him everywhere.

Then I discovered toddlers are not equipped with steering or brakes.

My image of taking him to the park and letting him run around the grass soon caved to the reality of having to herd him away from the trash-lined fence, as well as hover while he attempted to scale every picnic table and climb every slide. And the command, "Marcus, stop," usually resulted in hearing him laugh as he ran from me.

I've been thinking of this because I also had an image of worrying less about my son as he grew older. I've got to stop imagining things.

We were having dinner with friends recently, when their college freshman daughter called, in a panic. She was returning to campus in Santa Cruz, and had gotten on the train in San Jose, going in the wrong direction. Both parents bolted from their seats and ran off to help her.

I completely understood their distress, but I wondered what they were going to run off and actually do from Anaheim. When I got my own call a couple of weeks later, I knew why they had to jump and run.

Around 10 in the morning, I got a pre-recorded message from Cal State Long Beach. "This is to inform you that there has been a fatality on campus this morning," it said. "The name of the victim is being withheld until family can be notified."

It might have said a lot more, but my ears stopped listening at those first two sentences. Logically, I knew there are lots of people at Long Beach. I knew the chances of this being Marcus were very slim. And yet…

I sent him a text. "I can't help myself," I confessed. "You okay? Just got a canned message about a fatality at CSULB."

Of course, he didn't respond right away. I told myself it was because he has class at 10, and he's being a good student by paying attention to his professor instead of looking at his phone. Before I went back to cleaning, I reached out to my Facebook friends, asking if anyone would like to come and chain me to the house so I didn't race over to Long Beach and hunt down my son.

With that one phone call, I realized fear is able to transport a parent to their child, whether they're in Long Beach or San Jose.

An hour later, another phone call arrived, stating the accident victim was a female employee. My Facebook friends had already pointed me to some preliminary news on the internet. One of my son's friends commented on my status, worried about Marcus. I explained what happened and she wrote, "How many moms were given heart attacks?"

"All of them," I told her.

I'm still undecided whether the first phone call was necessary. If they'd waited an hour, they could have given more information and kept several thousand moms from frantically trying to reach their students. On the other hand, once news like this leaks out, it's probably best if the university tries to keep its community aware of what happened.

Marcus finally responded that he heard about the death as he walked past people at the bus stop. In other words, "don't stress, Mom."

I find myself longing for the days when falling off the slide was my biggest worry. He's negotiating a bigger world now, and I can only hope he's developed steering and brakes.

I CAN'T MISS YOU IF YOU DON'T LEAVE

By the time you read this, Marcus will be back at Cal State Long Beach, hard at work, making good grades, and setting a shining example of a solid and trustworthy college student.

That's my delusion and I'm sticking with it.

People often ask me if it's different now that he lives most of the year away from home. Do I miss him when he's gone? Or do I get tired of having him underfoot when he's home?

The answers are all "yes and no." Yes, I miss him when he's gone. He's very chatty and loves to show me the latest funny video on the Internet, or discuss important political issues. He's also very helpful, and I miss having an extra pair of hands to carry in the groceries and carry out the trash.

Having him around is also tiring, mostly because I have to keep reminding myself that he's not a child anymore and I can't just enforce rules because I'm the mom. If push came to shove, there are privileges like paying for his college and letting him have his car that we could threaten to withhold.

I'm not sure how serious the threats would be, though, since we'd like him to get a college education and his car makes our lives easier.

The worst thing about his being home is that it destroys my blissful ignorance of not knowing where he is. I know how strange that sounds, but once I became comfortable with the idea that I might as well trust him because I can't stalk him, I slept better.

We had a talk last summer after he got his car. I told him I realize he is 18 and I cannot forbid him to be out all night, or even decide he wants Oreos at 3 a.m. and go out to find some.

I did ask him to consider my sanity. If I know he's going to be out all night, I won't be listening for the garage door to open. If I think he's in bed, I don't want to hear what sounds like an intruder sneaking into my house.

He was mostly okay with this, although sometimes our communication skills need adjusting.

Last Sunday, I came home from grocery shopping and noticed his car was gone. I asked Dale where Marcus went.

"I don't know. He said he'd be right back."

That was around 6 p.m. By 8 p.m., dinner had been eaten an hour ago and there was still no Marcus. I sent him a text to ask where he was.

"Joe and Jakes. I'm in Long Beach helping them move a piano. It's raining so we are waiting."

I don't know how he thought he would be "right back" from that errand, but I watched a little TV, waiting to hear the garage door. At around 11:30 p.m., I sent another text. "Please shoot me a text if you are going to spend the night there."

He didn't respond, so I tried to assume he'd gotten the message and would text me. Then I went to bed and tried to sleep instead of wondering if he'd be okay on the rain-slicked streets.

The next morning, his car was in front of the house and my worry muscle relaxed. At that moment, I realized how much easier I would've slept if I didn't even know he'd been out.

Now that he's back at school, he could be moving a brass band and shopping for Oreos all night, but I'm okay with that.

Just don't tell me about it.

NOW I SEE HIM, NOW I DON'T

I'm learning that having a child in college is like running a small hotel on a lonely stretch of interstate highway. You spend a lot of nights with vacancies, then suddenly have a full house.

Marcus has been back at school since late January. Technically, I don't expect him to be home until spring break, which is next week. Realistically, he has a car and is only 20 miles away, so he could stop by the house at any time. According to him, he's overwhelmed in work, so he shouldn't have time to even leave the campus.

And yet, I'm sometimes surprised.

Last month, I let him know he had mail at our house and he indicated he would stop by and pick it up sometime. I put the envelope on the table, along with a Valentine's Day card from Dale and me, containing a gift card. I didn't tell him about the card, but I suspect his "starving student senses" were tingling.

At the time, I was in the middle of hyper-cleaning my house, in anticipation of company coming to spend the weekend with us. I love my family, but when I'm cleaning, I'd really prefer it if they go somewhere else, and possibly stay. I had already scrubbed the guest bathroom until it was squeaky, and had moved on to double-vacuuming the carpets in a vain attempt to remove all pet hair.

We had tickets to a play in La Mirada that Sunday, so I stopped cleaning, spruced myself up and went to the theater with my husband. When we got home, Marcus' car was parked in front of our house.

I walked into the house, expecting to see my son opening his mail, or making a sandwich, or playing with the dog. What I didn't expect to see was him emerging from my freshly cleaned bathroom with a towel around his waist.

"Why did you take a shower?" I asked.

"I was here. Shower was here. Might as well."

"Well, Sara and Mindy will be here on Friday, so make sure you clean up after yourself."

He gave me that "of course, Mom" look, no doubt because he thinks he always cleans up after himself. Before I had a chance to chat with him about his classes, friends, or dating life, he dressed and scampered back to Long Beach.

Our company came, had a great time, and returned to Sacramento, leaving our house with plenty of vacancies once again.

Two weeks later, I returned from grocery shopping on Sunday and tripped over a pile of dirty clothes by the washing machine. I recognized them as belonging to Marcus. My first thought was, is it spring break already? I found my son in the family room, working on his laptop, wearing a dress shirt and sweat pants.

"Is it spring break?" I asked.

"The washers at the dorm are all out of order."

I pointed to his outfit. "And this is all you had left?"

"Yep."

"Nice look. Are you staying for dinner?" I knew the answer to this question. What college student comes home and does not want to eat?

My normal Sunday meal tends to be grilled salmon with rice and vegetables. I usually buy salmon portions so there are no leftovers. Marcus was the luckiest son on the planet that Sunday, because I had decided at the last minute to fix turkey stir-fry instead.

A few hours later, I was left with an empty washer, dryer, and refrigerator. My small hotel was vacant again—until the next surprise visit.

IS THE DOG MORE ENTERTAINING THAN THE HUSBAND?

With Marcus moving to an apartment, our nest is feeling pretty empty these days. All I can talk about now is Dale or the dog.

I could ask Dale which he prefers, but I think I know the answer.

Some people treat their dogs like children. When my brothers and I were grown, our mother got a tiny black poodle to keep her company. Trying to keep us in the loop, she let us name it. Always the smart-alecky kids, we named the dog Kitty, so when you called, "Here Kitty," you'd get a poodle instead.

I don't know why my mother ever left us in charge of anything.

Kitty was spoiled so completely, she even trained our mom to feed her by hand. Trust me, Mom didn't lavish that kind of attention on us. We were expected to cut up our own meat.

After watching Kitty rule the roost, I couldn't treat a dog that way. I've loved all my dogs, but they eat out of a bowl, they sleep in a crate, and they do not wear dog clothes that have been made to look like they are little people.

I do, sometimes, treat Duffy to a spa day, if you call brushing and a bath a treat. It's not much of a treat for him, and it's no trip to Glen Ivy for me. I don't wash him often. Since he's at the ranch with me several days a week, it seems like a waste of time to bathe him, then turn him loose with a bunch of other dogs to play in the dirt.

He recently started shedding his winter coat. Corgis shed a lot every day, but twice a year they completely dump half of their hair in large clumps. The birds in our backyard love this. They use his discarded fur to build soft nests.

Of course, the mockingbirds don't wait that long. One of them teases Duffy from the front, while the mate snatches hair from his rump. Duffy does not like mockingbird nesting season.

Since he was shedding so much, I decided to give him a good brushing, followed by a bath. The brushing was an excellent idea. The jury is still out about the bath.

Duffy wasn't thrilled with the thirty minutes or so of heavy combing, during which time I pulled enough hair from him to stuff a couch, and possibly a matching love seat. After I had finished, he thought we were done. Imagine his surprise when I led him into the bathroom and told him to hop into the tub.

I was not surprised when he refused.

My experience at bathing dogs has taught me certain things. For example, after chasing previous pooches up and down the tub, I now put a leash on Duffy and tie it to the fixtures. He usually tries once to escape, then stands patiently while I lather and rinse him.

I just have to avoid his accusing stare. If he could talk, he'd tell me what a horrible owner I am. Then he'd call the ASPCA.

Bathing him after brushing him got him clean, but it also loosened the rest of the hair and dumped it, in the tub, on the towels, everywhere. Cleaning up was a nightmare. At one point, I wondered whether I would have to shave the bathroom to remove it all.

Eventually I had a clean dog and a hairless room, and no one was spoiled during the process.

Even Dale was happy, because it kept him out of the column.

WHEN DISTRACTIONS ARE INTERRUPTED

I used to think I was easily distracted. Many times, I've walked into a room to perform one task, only to do something else instead. Being a former engineer, I even make lists of the things I need to do, but it doesn't always help.

The list goes unfinished while the distractions get done.

Lately I've decided it's not that I'm easily distracted, it's that the distractions are hard to ignore. For example, I should put the groceries away before I re-organize the kitchen drawer, but if there was room in the drawer for the new bags I bought, then I wouldn't have to re-organize it.

In the past few weeks, I have not been able to make out a list or a schedule that didn't change by the minute. Dale informed me that our niece was going to come and stay with us for a month. This was fine, but I needed to do some serious housecleaning. I made my list of what needed to be done.

As if in protest, the distractions quickly began to mount. They started with an offer to refinance our house and take advantage of the lower interest rates. The offer was too good to ignore, and had to be started immediately. This meant I found myself searching through papers for last year's tax returns and standing at our temperamental fax machine, trying to patiently feed it 20 pages.

After that, came an entire category devoted to our son. He had signed up for classes next year, but hadn't told me that tuition was now due. Suddenly I got a panicked phone call that they'd cancelled his classes due to non-payment. Of course, I had to stop dusting the furniture to make certain he was re-enrolled.

A few days later, a similar call occurred. This time, it was about his rent payment. It seems both Marcus and his roommate are learning about the banking process. They thought an electronic transfer to the lease company would happen immediately. When the bank said it would take three days, it meant they would owe a late fee. Being good and responsible young men, this threw them into a tizzy.

Again, I stopped what I was doing so I could give him advice on what he might do. This included contacting the landlord, paying the late fees and planning ahead next month.

During this time, I also had a couple of days of multiple missed calls from Marcus. When you have two or three missed calls from your child, you generally treat that as life or death. It turns out, one call was to find out how long to cook spaghetti sauce, and one was to ask if coffee filters and grounds can be re-used.

I'm hoping to teach him to text me for these kinds of answers and save my adrenalin for emergencies.

Not wanting to feel left out, Dale also managed to pull me away from my plans. I received a text from him one morning asking if I'd seen his company-issued iPad. He didn't sound panicked, but I got a phone call a minute later.

"Did you find it?" he asked. "If it's not in the garage, look in the driveway. I might have left it on top of my car and driven off."

Now I was panicked. I dropped everything and went hunting. Fortunately, I found it in the garage, unharmed.

Eventually I got my original list completed. The house was clean enough for company. I would have liked to have done it with less distractions. But honestly, which one of those distractions should I have ignored?

SHATTERED DREAMS, BROKEN COFFEE POTS

It's hard to say goodbye to old friends, especially when they helped you through so much. At least, that's the way I feel about my appliances. I've lost a couple of them this year, and it's been tough.

First, I broke the carafe that went with my coffee maker. I guess you can't knock a glass container against the sink all the time without cracking it sooner or later.

In the old days, I used to go out and buy a new carafe. In the very old days, I even had a metal coffeepot because I kept breaking the glass ones. I had high hopes of doing the same thing. This is the future, when you can get anything you want, right?

Not when your coffee maker is twenty-five years old.

I searched all of our area stores. I looked online at Amazon. I even explored the coffee maker's company website. No one was selling pots without a machine, and the company doesn't even make coffee makers anymore.

It took me three weeks to do the research, narrow down my options, then refine them by whatever brand Target was selling. Although I was tempted to buy one of those makers that use the little pods and let you brew either a cup or a pot, in the end I went for the old fashioned kind that uses filters. I've heard that coffee grounds are good for my garden.

One of these days I should plant one.

The new coffee maker works great. I've gotten used to the insanely loud beep it makes to tell me the coffee is ready, and I'm being very careful when I wash the pot to keep it away from hard surfaces. More importantly, I had coffee again. Life was good.

Then yesterday the twenty-year-old slow cooker stopped working.

I had found a recipe online for a chicken stew made in the slow cooker that looked and sounded like hearty winter fare. Some of the ingredients were standard items around my house. The only things I needed were chicken thighs and stout beer.

I'm not a beer connoisseur. To me, lager is what they call a lumberjack in France. So I naively went to the store, looking for a single can of stout. Eventually I found a large bottle of "extra" stout. I hoped it would work.

One bottle and six thighs later, I was back in my kitchen. It took me half an hour to layer the slow cooker with meat and vegetables, then turn it on to "low." Before I left for the day, I checked the pot. It was hot.

At five o'clock, I was cold and hungry after teaching lessons at the ranch. All I had to do was add some frozen peas to the stew, then take a hot shower. Dinner would be ready when I was done.

I scampered through the house, lifted the lid on the pot and... it wasn't cooked all the way. The slow cooker was cool to the touch. I fiddled with the plug and the dial, but it wouldn't turn on.

While I moaned about ruined food, Dale came into the kitchen and said it was still on when he came home earlier, and that although the outside pot was cool, the inside crockery was still quite hot. I could see the meat was cooked, so I salvaged dinner.

Now I have to go out hunting for a new slow cooker. I hope my other appliances don't decide they've lived a full life yet. I'd hate to lose the toaster.

BECOMING A TWO-DOG HOUSE

As much as my family surprises me with their antics, sometimes I surprise myself more. I am an adult, and a former engineer, so I should be a model of prudent thinking and bullet-proof logic.

Why, then, did I just adopt another dog?

To be fair, I had been thinking about a second dog for a while, to give Duffy a playmate. My rational mind kept rejecting this idea. Two dogs meant twice the food, twice the vet bills, and at least twice the yard cleanup.

In addition, I was considering another Corgi puppy. Memories of housebreaking Duffy are still fresh enough in my mind to make me hesitate. I wasn't ready for another round of newspapers on the floor.

As luck would have it, the street where I board my horses has become a dumping ground for unwanted pets. I could spend an entire column ranting about this cruel practice, but I won't. It raises my blood pressure—why should I raise yours, too?

Most of the cats left on the street become coyote food, sadly. The dogs that don't get hit by a car sometimes find their way to our ranch, where my friend, the owner, tries to find either their owners or a new home. She is diligent about checking for I.D., even taking them to the vet to see if they've been micro-chipped.

It was no surprise to have a little red dog wandering around our street. She looked like a very petite Golden Retriever, wearing a faded collar that was several sizes too small. There were no tags, so my friend took her to the vet, checked the neighborhood for flyers, and called the pound to see if she was missing.

The vet found no chip on her, but estimated her to be at least 2 years old, 15 pounds overweight, and in need of serious grooming. Her hair was matted and covered in burrs. My friend gave her a good brushing and a bath, and looked around for either a good home or a good rescue organization.

I don't consider myself to be a "Golden Retriever person." I'm usually attracted to the herding breeds. I've seen enough Goldens to know they are overly energetic until they are 3 or 4, after which they settle down to being good, dependable dogs. Not necessarily smart dogs, but nice ones.

Still, this little Golden-mix caught my attention. Before I knew what I was doing, I took her home with me and Duffy.

The first 24 hours made me doubt my sanity. She was a basket case, panting, whining, and pacing everywhere. I took her on a walk, which calmed her a little, but not enough.

My first instinct was to try to find her another home, but I'm, at heart, a stubborn woman and don't give up that easily. By the second day, I was trying to figure out a name for her. I thought of many sweet names, like Dolly, Merry, and Lucy, but none of them seemed to stick.

After day three, I decided there was no use trying to pin a dignified name on this licking, panting beast. I might as well call her what I'd been calling her since she came home: Spazz.

It's been a week now, and Spazz is settling down into a more agreeable dog. She has stopped pacing and panting, and Duffy enjoys playing with her. Of course, I don't know if my house will survive their wrestling matches.

We've also given her a more dignified name, Lady Spazzleton.

Adopting Spazz was probably not the most logical choice I could have made. But what's wrong with surprising yourself?

WHO AM I MARRIED TO?

When it comes to spouses, if you've been married any length of time, you feel that you know everything about them, and they know everything about you. Or they should know. One of the funniest lines for any marriage counselor is when one partner says, "We've been married for 25 years, they should know how I feel."

Dale and I have been married for 21 years, and I confess, I've come to expect certain behaviors from him. He is quiet but friendly, and difficult to rattle. He is also a straight shooter. When I tell a story, he is quick to point out when I am exaggerating.

I can only get away with that in my column.

As plain-spoken as Dale is, a couple of recent incidents have made me question whether I know him, and how well. The first one happened at a conference I attended last weekend.

Each February, I spend three days with other writers at a conference, teaching workshops and getting my creative batteries recharged. Dale usually joins me on Saturday night for the banquet. A large group of us end up in the bar, talking and laughing for a few hours more.

Last Saturday, a friend of mine was complimenting me on my skin. "I don't believe you're 50."

"I'm well over that," I said.

Dale looked across the table at her, a serious expression on his face. "You'd never know she was 65," he said.

For the record, he's exaggerating.

All I could do was burst into a laughter so raucous, it turned heads. Who knew my husband was capable of taking me by such surprise?

After the conference, I came home to real life which included everything from doing laundry to celebrating my birthday. My girlfriends treated me to dinner on Tuesday. It was a lovely get together.

It was also the night of torrential rainstorms. I drove home slowly, through the flooded streets. When I arrived I ran from my minivan to the front door, wishing I had not sacrificed my side of the garage to general storage. Dale was in the bedroom, watching TV.

"Man, it's wet out there," I told him.

"We had a flash flood."

This shocked me. Our house is on very flat land on a very flat street. "Where?"

"Here." He waved his hands around.

"But what flooded?"

"We did." He was insistent, and seemingly annoyed that we were having this conversation.

We've had this kind of discussion before, where we both think we are talking about something and it turns out it is not the same something. I tried, once more, to get on the same page as my husband. Perhaps our pool had overflowed, or our yard could not absorb the water fast enough and had dumped the excess toward the patio.

"Did water get into our house somehow? Because I think of a flood as water rising from the ground—" I stopped. That didn't make sense. "You know, it rains down hard enough that it fills the ground up." Now I was waving my hands around.

"No, it was a flash flood, you know, when rain comes down really hard. It's the hardest I ever heard. We even lost the satellite once."

I finally had some idea what he was talking about. For me, a flood requires covering a portion of the Earth with too much water. For Dale, a large amount of rain pouring down is enough.

Once again, my husband caught me by surprise. After being married for 21 years, should he know how often he does this?

CLEAN AND SHINY, THE WAY I LIKE IT

Please forgive any errors in today's column. I've been cleaning house all week and my fingers are all wrinkled and dry from the scrubbing. I suppose I could wear gloves, but I thought dermabrasion was good for your skin.

In the meantime, it's like typing with hands wrapped in newspaper.

Spring cleaning is a common ritual, and I can understand how it all got started. Having grown up in the Midwest, I remember the long winter months of closed windows and the constant hum of the furnace. Most people kept their houses warm enough to be comfortable in shorts. Between the cold, wet air outside and the hot, dry air inside, it's a wonder we didn't all have perpetual pneumonia.

It was also impossible to keep us kids from tracking snow or mud through the house, at least according to my grandmother. Add to this the fact that all the men in my family were smokers and I'm sure you can imagine my house after four months of winter weather.

Throwing the windows open on that first warm day made you feel like celebrating. Okay, it made me feel that way. It made my grandmother feel like washing every bedspread and curtain.

If I stood still too long, she'd wash me, too.

As I grew up and lived on my own, my grandmother's clean gene blossomed in me, so that every spring, I also went on a housework binge. I washed the knick-knacks and steam-cleaned the sofas. Bookshelves were emptied, dusted, and re-organized, as were the music collections.

This week, as I balanced the range top on my shoulders to scrub the grout and tile I can never reach under the lip of its metal frame, I had a thought. Why am I still driven to clean the house each spring in southern California?

It's not like I spent the winter suffocating in a closed, overheated house. As a matter of fact, I'm known to open the windows in January, just to hear the rain better. It has nothing to do with any hot flashes I might be having.

Still, I am compelled to clean the house every spring. Not that I don't clean the house at other times, more or less, here and there. But around March, my brain starts getting muddled and I find myself irritable and restless. There are things I'd rather be doing, things like working on a novel, riding my horses, or taking ukulele lessons, but I'm in such a funk I can't even buy the uke.

The only cure is to scrub and dust and vacuum.

After stocking my house with soaps, wipes, sponges, and Advil, I've spent three days getting re-acquainted with the nooks and crannies of my house. The first thing I discovered was, now that we have two dogs and a cat, the carpet under my sofa has missed me and the vacuum.

I've still got a couple of days' worth of cleaning to do. The bookcases definitely need to be re-done, and I'm guessing that the Placentia Library's Friends Bookstore will benefit from my efforts. It's also been a long time since I cleaned out the DVDs, so they will probably also be weeded out. It's a lot of work, but the payoff is worth it.

The next time you see me, I'll be a calmer, more focused person with neat shelves and clean carpets. I might even own a ukulele.

REALITY 101

I get interesting texts from Marcus. In their simplicity, they make me think about complex issues. It started with this message:

"Mom, what is the best way to resolve a going flat tire?"

After I decided this wasn't a trick question, I answered him. "Put air in it. Then drive over to Allen's garage."

"He knows what to do," one of my friends told me. "He just wants you to do it."

Marcus tries to be self-sufficient, but sometimes he does have a passive way of getting me to do things for him. I started thinking about other things we've had to teach our son. From budgeting money to basic cooking, I knew he would not receive these life skills in any class.

Things are different from when I went to school. When I was a mere child (and dinosaurs roamed the Earth) we had to take classes that would prepare us for more than high school graduation. Our school system knew we didn't have a lick of common sense, so they taught us home economics, wood shop, and how to write a check.

Of course, being the 60s, the girls were in the kitchen and the boys were in the shop, but at least we learned to boil water and hammer a nail. And we all knew how to spend money.

As wonderful as I think our Placentia Yorba Linda School District is, I know that they are at the mercy of funding. I've seen the kind of juggling our officials have to do to keep a balanced curriculum that will prepare our kids for their future. Still...

If I ruled the world, I'd have a class called Reality 101. Students would learn to do laundry and clean a bathroom, to shop for groceries and prepare a meal, and that cars need oil and coolant. They'd also be taught about loans and credit cards, especially if they go to college. Passing this class would be required for graduation.

It's already required for life.

I was discussing this with my friend, and she said, "That would have been a good class when I was in school." She then told me the story of letting her car run completely out of oil because she didn't know it needed it.

"Maybe I should have read the manual," she admitted.

I thought about that. "It might not have helped. The manuals all have diagrams that point to where the oil goes, but I don't know of any statement that your car will die without it. I think they just assume everyone knows a car needs stuff to run."

I only know what a car needs because I took Driver's Education in high school, and we had to learn about the internal combustion engine as part of the course. It was the hardest class I ever took, and the only C I received. Cars were, and are, a mystery to me.

I'm still surprised when I look under the hood and there's no squirrel on a treadmill.

I asked Marcus if his driver training class taught him about the parts of the car. He said no, but somewhere along the way he figured out that cars need oil and coolant. This would make me feel better if he hadn't sent me the following text recently:

"The check engine light is on in my car."

Yes, I had to tell him to take it to Allen again. The good news is, he seems to be learning Reality 101. The bad news is, he still expects me to fix it for him.

THE SATELLITE COMPANY IS SENDING ME INTO ORBIT

If you've read this column for a few years, you know my difficulties in getting repairmen to my home in a timely manner. And from your emails, I know I'm not alone in this.

For several weeks I've been getting notices from both my internet provider and my satellite company about needing to upgrade. My internet provider has a new service. The satellite company has new programming. I have old equipment.

Both companies insist that, like death, taxes and the Borg, these upgrades are inevitable and resistance is futile.

At last, I surrendered and ordered the service calls. Being a glutton for punishment, I ordered both updates for the same day. What could go wrong?

The day before the appointment, I decided not to make the technicians wade through dog hair and dust to get to our equipment, so I spent the day mopping, dusting, and vacuuming. Since they had to replace a receiver in our bedroom, I even did five loads of laundry and put all the clothes away.

Even I was impressed.

Mario, the internet guy, was the first to arrive. Since he didn't need access to the backyard, I stuck the dogs there. He reviewed my order with me, then told me he had to go down the street and disable my phone service.

Uh-oh.

The satellite company had not called to confirm their appointment, and I could not remember if I had given them my cell phone number as a backup. As if on cue, the phone rang and a recorded message from the satellite company asked if today was still good for me.

I had just enough time to say, "yes" before the connection died.

Mario was fiddling with my phone jack when the satellite man, Brett, showed up. He did need access to the backyard, so I did the only thing I could think of with the dogs. I put them on leashes and hauled them around the house. They were confused and kept pulling toward the front door for a walk.

As I watched Brett evaluating our satellite dish and the tangle of cables running around our eaves, I started to wonder. I had requested replacements for two of our three receivers. Why was he staring at my roof?

"I'm going to have to re-locate your new dish," he said.

This was the beginning of a very long conversation.

"What new dish?"

After ten minutes of animated discussion, we finally figured out what happened. I believed I was only upgrading the two receivers that were obsolete. The satellite company believed I was getting a new HD dish with two brand new receivers. I don't know what they expected me to do with the third one in our house, which would now be useless.

Unlike my grandmother, who once knocked out an entire wall in her house while Grandpa was at work, I like to talk over changes to our home with Dale first. I put the order on hold until we could investigate what this would do to our budget.

"You know, you don't have to replace anything," Brett said. "Your current equipment will work just fine."

Even without all the work being accomplished, I still considered the day successful. The internet upgrade was working great, and I had time to look into the whole satellite thing.

Then the next day I got an email from the satellite company. I need to replace my receivers or I'll lose programming. Maybe I can get Brett back before I have to vacuum again.

CHANNELING MY GRANDMOTHER

One of the nice things about raising our children is noticing which side of the family they look like, and which side they act like. This is a fun game, until we look in the mirror and see our mothers looking back at us. Then it gets scary.

This may be a female phenomenon. I don't hear a lot of men discussing how much they resemble their dads. They may not even notice it, or if they do, they're not admitting it.

Apart from my red hair and overbite, I look more like the women on my dad's side of the family, although I certainly don't see my dad when I look in the mirror. I even share the same body shape as my dad's mom and sisters.

Recently, however, I'm starting to see similarities in my actions to another member of the family, one on my mom's side.

I am turning into my grandma.

This realization began to emerge yesterday, when I had to take my car in for routine service. I am currently helping a friend of mine from Australia with a project for her school class, by taking a poster about recycling, designed by the kids, around to various locations and snapping pictures of it. Of course, I got pictures next to the Placentia Civic Center sign, but I thought Disneyland would be perfect for the kids abroad.

I just needed someone to help me take photos, so I came up with a great solution: Marcus could pick me up at Allen's garage and drive us to Disneyland, where we would take some photos before the park got too hot and crowded.

We got there before huge waves of people arrived, but there was definitely a steady stream of families milling through Downtown Disney toward the parks.

Let me first say that no one in my family walks together anywhere. We all kind of scatter, then re-group as we move down a sidewalk. Marcus in particular likes to walk behind me, right at my shoulder. As we walked along, I kept shifting over to get through clumps of people who were not moving.

"Mom, you're worse than walking with the dogs," my son finally told me. "You keep wandering away, then walking in front of me."

We ducked into a store, because he was looking for a new pair of sunglasses. This particular store sold sunglasses and handbags. It didn't take me long to start going through all the bags, looking inside, holding them up, and talking to the salesclerk about what I needed in a new purse.

I looked up to see Marcus at the entrance, waiting.

Suddenly a vision came to me, of a spry little woman wandering about while we tried to keep up with her, then spending hours in a store looking at everything in it.

As we returned home, I told him, "Get used to this. Someday when I'm in my 80s, you'll have to take me to the store and you'll tell all your friends, 'man, it takes forever to take my mom shopping. She wanders up and down every aisle and has to handle every can on the shelf.'"

"Nah," he said.

I'm not certain whether he meant I would not drive him crazy, or whether he's planning to pay someone else to take me shopping.

As far as turning into my grandmother, I could do a lot worse. She was never bored, young at heart, and told wonderful stories. If I can have half of her liveliness, I'll be a happy old lady.

OODLES OF APPLES

I like our neighbors. While we don't see much of them, we have really pleasant families on both sides of our house. We smile, we wave, we stop and chat.

Lately, we've had a little problem with one of our neighbor's trees. They have an apple tree that is producing bushels of nice looking apples this year. The branches extend over into our yard, which under normal circumstances would be lucky for us. I doubt if they would mind if we helped ourselves to the ones that fall on our side.

There is only one problem.

Our retriever-muppet mix, Lady Spazzleton loves to eat apples. She treats them like manna from heaven, possibly sent to her as some kind of reward for not chewing any more seat belts. Being a typical dog, she has no appestat to tell her she's had enough. She doesn't know when she's had enough of anything.

Much like myself and Oreos.

At first, I let her eat the apples. There were only a couple on the ground—or so I thought. It turns out, there were a lot of apples on the ground, and she ate all of them.

The following morning, I discovered why this was a bad idea. Spazz's tummy had been upset during the night. It was so upset that I had a very unpleasant surprise in the family room where she sleeps.

Make that five or six unpleasant surprises.

Both dogs spent the morning in the yard while I cleaned up, after I had picked up the remaining apples. Once the carpets were scrubbed, I let the dogs back in. Spazz came in with her head down and something in her jaws. She had found another apple.

I reached down for it and she growled a little, so I grabbed the scruff of her neck and gave her a stern shake. She dropped the apple and, still angry with me, attacked Duffy. Duffy's no lightweight, so soon I had a full-scale dogfight in my kitchen. I pulled Spazz's tail and reached for Duffy's collar. Unfortunately, I missed his collar, but he didn't miss my hand with his teeth.

Now I had a dogfight and a bloody finger.

The dogs were not going to stop, so I got the rake from the yard and hit them both in the head with the handle. They jumped apart and looked at me as though I'd awakened them from a dream.

My lesson learned, the next time Spazz wandered in with an apple, I didn't try to take it away from her. Instead, I called to Duffy to put him in another room. Duffy is no fool. He knew that Spazz was being disciplined, and felt he was just the dog to give her a spanking.

This time, I hit them with a yardstick.

Thus has begun my mission to keep apples away from Spazz without having to break up World War Doggie. The yard is checked for apples each morning. If she snags one, misdirection is now applied

I act like I don't notice, throw the ball for Duffy to chase into one room and close the door. I then take the apple from Spazz and throw a ball for her. Everyone has a ball and no one has to get spanked.

I've considered asking the neighbors if we could trim the branches on our side, but there are a lot of branches and I'd hate to kill their tree. I may not be getting along with my dogs, but I want to stay on my neighbors' good side.

COOKING—IT'S IN THE DNA

I have fond childhood memories of sitting on my grandmother's counter while she whipped up some kind of delicious food. Sometimes it was chicken and noodles, sometimes it was a pie, but it usually involved giving me a glob of dough to knead while she rolled out the rest. I'd like to say that she taught me to cook, but mostly I just played with my piece of dough while we talked about everything.

Regrettably, I do not know how to make her wonderful pie crust because I was too busy asking her how spiders potty.

When Marcus was little, I didn't teach him a lot about cooking. Before you accuse me of being sexist, I wouldn't have taught a daughter much more. I don't cook like Grandma did. He knew how to get a bowl of cereal, make a sandwich, and use the microwave.

It's possible I considered my job to be done at that point.

He did help me decorate Christmas cookies one year. As usual, I had my big forest of sugar cookie trees, which needed green icing and a few sprinkles. Honestly, I tried to be a hands-off mom, but it was difficult to keep reminding him not to lick icing from his fingers, then handle the cookies.

Now that he's lived on his own, his cooking has expanded. He can scramble eggs, fix spaghetti, and even makes bread from scratch. I'm impressed, although his pasta-making continues to baffle me, since he always makes the entire amount that he purchases. This means, if he buys a two-pound box, he fixes a mountain of spaghetti.

I once asked him why he didn't just fix what he needs. He gave me That Look.

"Sooner or later, I'll eat it all."

Last night I decided to broaden his culinary skills. "Want to learn to make stuffed bell peppers?" I asked. He was playing an online game with his friends, so I thought the answer would be a polite, "I'd love to but I'm in the middle of something."

Instead, I got an enthusiastic, "Yes, I'll be right there."

The first step was to chop up an onion. It's amazing to watch my son try to cut anything up. This is the young man who can carry all of the groceries from the car in a single trip. Yet each slice of the knife seems to take all his strength.

After a while, we had large, irregular-shaped pieces of onion to sauté. With each step, he was enthusiastic, if not always coordinated. We got the peppers in the oven and he went back to his game.

As I waited for the timer, I posted on Facebook about teaching my son to make stuffed peppers, adding that he is available. Marcus never has anything to say about my posts, but he was out of his room within moments.

"I hear you're auctioning me off," he said.

"All I said was," I replied, and told him.

"Nah, it's okay, they said it was totally cute."

"When are my posts not totally cute?"

"Never, Mom." He went back to his game.

Not only did he have the right answer, the peppers turned out great. I may not know how to make pie crust, but at least I can pass some skills on to my son. Cooking and communication never go out of style.

CHANGING HORSES IN MID-AFTERNOON

Like any busy gal, my calendar is full of activities for each day. They say we plan and God laughs. I would like to add that my family gets a few giggles in as well when I try to plan anything.

This past Sunday, I had to be at the McCoy Center in Chino Hills to help my trainer at a horse show. We had 10 students and 5 horses to wrangle, and at these shows, there is much wrangling to be done. The children ranged in age from 8 to 16. They were a fun group, but it was a lot of work, too.

In between pinning numbers on shirts and answering questions, we also had to get the horses ready. Horses tend to be homebodies, and it makes them nervous to go to a strange place where everything looks different.

Fortunately, the horses were easy to calm down. We just exercised them to make them tired. The children could not be run around in circles, so we had to keep telling them they'd be fine. We spent the day trying to remember which child rode which horse in what class. Once we got a pair into the class, we stood along the fence and prayed that the horse did its job, instead of running away with the child.

Five hours later, the show was done. Everything was a success. No one fell off, and no one cried because they didn't win. As I drove back to Placentia, the stress of being responsible for these kids finally left me, and I realized I was exhausted.

The next thing on my plan was to return home, eat lunch and shower, with plenty of relaxation before, during, and after. I didn't put it on my calendar, but if I did, it would have said, "Relax after working tushie off."

I had completed the part about going home and eating when I got the text from Dale. His brother and family were visiting from Oregon, and they were on their way to our house.

Dale has three wonderful brothers, all with delightful families, and I love to spend time with them. But all I could think of when he texted me was, "Oh, no. The house is a mess. I'm a mess. I can't see people right now. It's not in my plan."

I was showered, but still out of sorts when Dale got home. He was a little cranky that I was cranky, so I did my best to rally. I put all my plans of relaxation aside and happily greeted our guests.

My sister-in-law is one of those women who can walk past my dirty dishes and not even blink. She actually laughed when I cleaned up the dining room so they could have their dinner. We had a nice chat, in between chasing my two young grandnieces about.

I somehow ended up entertaining the little girls. Marcus still has a number of his more interactive books, so we read about bugs and dinosaurs. The girls wanted a story about a princess, but all I could offer was a frog in a tiara. Frogs do not make good princesses, by the way.

They only stayed a couple of hours, which was unlike them, but it was a good visit, and afterward, I finally got my dose of relaxation. As it turns out, it was on the schedule after all. My family had just penciled it in for later.

PARENTAL POP QUIZZES

They say children keep us young. I don't know who "they" are, but I don't think "they" have kids. Yes, it's fun to watch them discover life in all their innocence. But I'm pretty certain their excitement over testing their own skills extends into testing their parents' abilities.

Our reflexes are put to the test most often. Children love to measure how long they can misbehave before we stop them.

They also like pop quizzes. I remember many blurry-eyed mornings when Marcus would hand me a sheet of paper as we got into the minivan.

"This is for today's field trip," he'd say.

I'd mumble, dig a pen out of my purse and start writing.

I understand that field trip forms need an amount of legal-sounding words saying they'll do their best to return my child in one piece, but I always felt like I was applying for a mortgage. The information I had to supply seemed endless, and coincidentally, was the same information I wrote out in triplicate at the beginning of each school year.

Between you and me, I often made up the doctor's phone number and address. After all, the school had the correct information, they were going to call me first anyway, and I was filling this out at the stop light before turning into the Morse Elementary School parking lot.

I thought those days were over, but they have just morphed into another challenge.

Ever since Marcus has been in college, I have told him to let me know when he signs up for classes so I can pay the tuition. On more than one occasion, he signed up and forgot to tell me. This meant his classes got cancelled, I was locked out of paying for anything for about a week, and everyone was stressed.

This year, I thought I'd be smart. I logged onto his account and saw tuition was due, so I paid it and sent him the obligatory "You were supposed to tell me" text.

On Friday, I got this message from him: "I got an email saying I owe $1100 by Wednesday or they're cancelling my classes."

What did I just pay? After a lot of texting, he agreed to go to the finance office on Monday to figure it out. Monday afternoon, I contacted him to see what he discovered.

"I've been sick so I pretty much slept all day. I'll have time to do it tomorrow," he replied.

I was sorry about his cold, but leaving it until the day before payment was due amped my stress level. The next day I texted again, in the late afternoon, hoping for a better response.

"I'm in line at the cashier's office now. I'll let you know."

Did I mention it was late afternoon?

After another round of texting, we figured it out. Although he had signed up for all his classes, he was wait-listed for some. He was only officially enrolled in enough courses to make him a part-time student. Once the wait-listed classes showed him as enrolled, we were hit with the rest of the bill.

You could say I should have known I wasn't paying full tuition. You could also suggest that we just put money into his account and let him assume the responsibility. You could recommend lots of remedies to get us through the next couple of semesters without so much drama.

I'd probably reject the help, though. These little tests may drive me crazy, but I'm used to them. Someday, I hope to pass one.

HOW CAN CHILDREN BE GETTING YOUNGER IF I'M NOT GETTING OLDER?

Is it me or are children looking younger lately? I left home early the other day and had to wait for several students to cross the street. They were on their way to Kraemer Middle School, but they were so small, I wondered if they weren't third-graders on a field trip to the big kids' school.

When Marcus attended Kraemer, I thought he and his friends looked very grown up. Why, they were practically adults in my mind, except for the part where they were incapable of making good decisions.

Of course, he did age as he progressed through his high school years. All of the kids did. I thought they couldn't get any older looking. If they did, it would mean I was getting older, too.

Now, of course, I see how silly I was. From his facial hair to his lanky frame, "college" Marcus definitely looks more adult than "high school" Marcus. And his "college" mom is different from his "high school" mom.

Last Friday, I was invited to Valencia High School, to be a judge at their talent show. This show wasn't held for a few years, mostly due to the tremendous amount of effort it takes to host. It was resurrected when Marcus was a senior and proved to be a big hit, both for the kids who wanted to express themselves and for the departments that needed a fundraiser.

Megan Arthurton, the choir director, asked me to judge for a couple of reasons. One is that we are friends and, with our busy schedules, it's one of the few times a year we can actually see one another. The other is that I have no children at VHS, so I can be fair and impartial.

I showed up and watched the kids getting ready. They all had baby faces, but I tried to remind myself that many of these "kids" were already 18 and considered adults, at least by legal standards.

Maybe it's because I'm a mom, but the law seems more lenient than I am.

My two fellow judges, both VHS teachers, looked young as well. They were well-versed in popular music. I was glad, since my interest in all things popular has waned. I'm not going to blame this on my age. I'll let others do that.

As soon as the lights dimmed, the voices in the crowd rose. Megan managed to contain the audience's enthusiasm, briefly. When the first performers took the stage, the uproar started again.

I reminded myself that this is the norm for high school events. Having been to four years of concerts at Cal State Long Beach, I've grown used to spectators that are mostly quiet and attentive to the performers.

The crowd was still screaming when the singer began. I worried that they would continue to shriek for the entire song. I wouldn't be able to judge what I couldn't hear. Sooner or later, the audience quieted and I was able to fulfill my duty. These screams were repeated for each act.

At last it was over and the judges gathered in a corner to discuss our scores and determine a winners for each category. We were mostly in agreement, and were able to pick winners without any debate or arm-wrestling.

Once again, I was happy to be of service to Valencia. I can only hope that next year, these kids don't look even younger. I'd hate to think I was that much older.

WE REMEMBER THE GOOD TIMES

My horse trainer's little boy is in preschool, which means he is bringing home an equal amount of cute drawings and bad colds, all of which he shares with his parents. His mom is now referring to him as Typhoid Tyler.

One particularly hard week, Niki was complaining, in between coughs, about her muscle aches from sleeping with her son on the couch. As usual, I tried to reassure my friend that I went through the same thing with Marcus and survived.

I thought back to my days as the mother of a two-year-old. "Here's the thing," I told her. "I know Marcus got sick, and I know it was worrisome and frustrating, but I don't have a lot of real memories about it. I only remember the good stuff."

"Is this like that thing where you forget how painful childbirth is and you decide to have another one?" she replied.

It may be true. The only thing I really remember about all the illnesses is that my son had a gag muscle that belonged in the Guinness Book of Records. He could projectile medicine further than most missile launchers.

He also had an interesting way of interpreting his own sickness. Sometimes he would announce, "My throat hurts." I quickly learned this was the 30-second countdown before he threw up.

I also learned why loft-style beds are not always a good choice for kids when their throats hurt.

The biggest illness Marcus ever had was chicken pox. Although we had him vaccinated, we found out the vaccine tended to lose its protectiveness after 10 years or so. He was 12 and getting ready for a soccer game when he showed me the itchy, red dot on his side. I confirmed my suspicions with the Dial-a-Nurse help line.

Dale was sympathetic. He was also Marcus' coach. "Is he really that contagious?"

Treating an itchy 12-year-old may sound easy, but I was ready to tape oven mittens to his hands by the time it was over. In addition, I had to fight off the neighbors, who were all clamoring to get their children in the same toxic space as my son so they could get the pox and get it over with.

Now that Marcus is all grown up and living on his own, I don't have to force Children's Tylenol down his throat, but I do learn about his various ailments through the wonders of text messaging.

Last month, he asked if I could think of any way to completely clear up a cough. He had a singing gig and a lingering cold, two things that don't mix well. I recommended several medicines that could clear up his post-nasal drip, plus plenty of water and lozenges.

He decided on cough syrup, nasal spray, and sang the entire concert with a lozenge in his cheek. I know this because I was there. It was a half-hour set, and he was great.

I know this because I'm his mom.

After a trip to Urgent Care, plus a week of sleep deprivation and wrestling a toddler to the ground to stuff medicine in him, my trainer is happy to report Typhoid Tyler has made a full recovery. This week, he started a new preschool and will soon be bringing a new drawing home for Mom to hang on the fridge.

I'll give her a few years before she forgets the illness and only remembers the good times.

WHEN THE UNIVERSE LAUGHS, LAUGH ALONG

There are some days when I don't know whether the Universe is trying to make me laugh or cry. Maybe it's a little bit of both.

On Monday, Dale's car battery died. Being a Do-It-Yourself kind of guy, he took my car to the store to buy a replacement.

"Your car is idling rough," he said upon his return.

My minivan is 17 years old and has almost 240,000 miles on it. It has developed a few quirks over time. I figured this was a new one. That is, until I tried driving to the ranch in Chino Hills on Tuesday. At each traffic light, the entire van panted like my dogs on a summer day.

Car trouble was the last thing I needed. Formulating a quick plan to cancel my 9 o'clock lesson, and somehow get to the ranch later, I drove immediately to Allen's garage and told him my van was panting.

"Of course it is," he said, and popped the hood.

A small hose had become loosened. Allen put a clamp on it, assured me that it would keep my van operational, and sent me on my way.

Thinking I had seen the worst of the day, I drove down Lambert and entered the canyon. For anyone who hasn't driven route 142 through Carbon Canyon, it's a little over 10 miles of narrow, winding road. Two trucks were ahead of me, both pulling trailers with new windows, going somewhere to be installed. At the sharpest switchback, the trucks slowed, as I expected.

Then they stopped.

I pulled up behind them and saw the problem. In the opposite lane, a small grey compact had crossed into the oncoming traffic and plowed into a large white SUV. The SUV won.

The accident had just happened, apparently, and there was no one from law enforcement to direct anyone's movements, so we were all trying to get by without causing another crash. I would have given up and gone home, but there was no place to turn around. At last, I managed to slip past the wreckage.

Once I got to the ranch, my day returned to normal. The Universe may not have wanted me to get there, but nothing bad was waiting for me once I persevered.

After a day of teaching and riding, I headed for home, tired and wanting a shower. My gas tank was very low, so I decided to stop and fill up. The station near my house was busy, but I pulled up behind a car and waited my turn.

The customer ahead of me was washing his back window with the squeegee. As he stepped to the side, I saw that the pump nozzle was not in his car. Then I watched him apply the squeegee to the entire back of his car and wipe the whole thing down with paper towels. He looked at me and shrugged.

Another pump opened up, so I took it. As I filled my van, I continued to watch the man, who basically washed his entire car with the squeegee and kept everyone else from using that pump. He was still washing when I drove away.

I suppose I could have been annoyed, but it was the darnedest thing I'd seen all day. The Universe may have slapped me awake this morning, but it wrapped up the day with a laugh.

THE PERKS OF THE OLDER MOM

When Marcus was born, I was "the older mom." This meant a lot more tests at the doctor, and some interesting conversations with strangers. I can still recall that first day at the park when a woman asked me if Marcus was my only grandchild.

It wasn't the last time.

Now I'm watching other "older moms" having their first babies and I'm reliving my glory days as a sleep-deprived woman with a diaper bag in one arm and a screaming child in the other.

My horse trainer and I were at lunch recently, discussing her son. He will be three in July and is already such a little man, talking in complete sentences and wanting to do everything by himself.

"How did he get that old?" she asked me.

"Ask me that again when he's 21," I told her. "I still have a memory of holding Marcus as a baby."

I put my hands up to simulate the way I used to hold Marcus and, for a moment, felt the weight of him again, snuggled against me. Niki nodded and held her hands up, too. We sat there, wondering how time passes.

The years flashed across my brain as we talked. I saw a glimpse of me following Toddler Marcus around a public place, then tagging Dale, who took over the next lap. There were moments of Little Boy Marcus to Young Man Marcus, all of which I savored.

As I remembered holding my baby, I realized how happy I am to have that physical memory, and how much I would miss it if it slipped away. I also realized, suddenly I wanted to see my very grown-up son on Sunday.

It's no secret that Mother's Day is not usually a big deal for me. Eating a meal I didn't cook, and spending the day loafing works. I don't always get to see or hear from my son, and that's okay, too. Whoever decided May was a great time for Mother's Day and college final exams was clearly not thinking.

Or maybe they aren't a mom.

Normally, I try to get Dale and Marcus to coordinate the whole Mother's Day thing. After all, their personal assistant should have one day off. This year I knew what I wanted, so there was no sense trying to hint around.

By the way, I'd really like to meet the woman who is able to get what she wants by hinting to a man. That gal could be the next President.

I contacted Marcus in the only way I knew he'd get the message—by Facebook. "Are you available any time this Sunday?" I asked. "For Mother's Day I'd like to meet you for a meal. Any meal, any time."

We moms aren't too proud to beg.

He told me he was free in the morning and early afternoon. I chose afternoon and told him we'd meet him somewhere in Long Beach.

"Whatever you want, Mom," he told me. "It's Mother's Day."

On the minus side, I won't be able to hold him against me and rock him to sleep. On the plus side, I won't be chasing him through the restaurant, either. I will, however, be able to share a meal with my son. And I don't care if I'm the older mom. If you wait long enough, no one asks anymore.

PREPARING FOR THE MINIVAN'S RETIREMENT

It's no secret that I am a stubborn woman. I prefer the term "motivated", or perhaps "determined", but it means the same thing. Abandoning a project or a goal is not acceptable.

This is how I get stuck all day trying to install software on my computer. If something goes wrong, I can't give up.

My minivan is one thing I am obstinate about. I've loved it ever since I drove it home one Sunday afternoon. I had gone out to get groceries in my Honda Prelude, and I came back with a minivan instead.

"I knew you were going to get one, but I didn't know it was today," was all Dale said about it.

It has always been the right size, spacious on the inside and maneuverable on the outside. Its only dents have come from the misjudgment of others. Inside, it was anointed within the first week by a crayon Marcus left for me on the front seat.

I wish I would have known about it before it sat in the sun all day and melted into the fabric. I also wish that was the worst thing the upholstery was anointed with.

In the years that followed, the minivan toted our family on vacations, and Marcus' friends to various school activities. We even drove it to Illinois and back one summer on a rather epic journey to visit my brother.

Seventeen years later, the van no longer carries Marcus and his friends around, but I still enjoy the spaciousness of it when I'm taking my saddle and various tack to horse shows, or my boxes of books and tables to an author's festival.

Sometimes I even have a combination of the horse stuff and books to schlep around.

I love my van so much, I vowed publically to keep driving it until it had 300k miles on it. Secretly, though, I resolved to drive it forever. I figured my mechanic Allen could just keep replacing anything that broke due to old age. New cars bring higher insurance and registration fees, anyway. And if I bought a new car, I'd want another minivan.

The van now has 243k miles, and my determination to keep it is being tested. Allen can still replace what breaks, but the breakage is costing more each time. My last bout with car trouble started with a small coolant leak that was traced to a hose at the firewall.

Many hoses later, it was not a cheap fix.

"Maybe I should start looking for a new car," I told Dale, even though I hated saying it.

"It's up to you," he said. "Just get your money's worth out of the last repair."

I love that my husband thinks I am a smart, capable woman, but every once in a while, I'd like him to be just a little opinionated.

After arguing with myself for a week or so, I finally came up with a compromise. Instead of my original goal, I'll start looking for a new car when I have 250k miles, or another major repair, whichever comes first.

That gives me seven thousand miles to prepare myself to say goodbye to my minivan and replace it with something else. Yes, I realize that the van may break down before I reach that goal. But if I can't be stubborn, at least I can be optimistic.

GOD IS MY CAR DEALER

I think anyone who believes in God, or any Supreme Being, has tried to bargain with their Deity. In exchange for granting one request, they will either never do what they shouldn't, or always do what they should.

For students, these deals are made during finals week.

I'm also guilty of bargaining with God. God's reaction is probably to shake His head and wonder why I think He won't take care of me, and then sit back and laugh.

My latest plea involved the minivan. I wanted to get another 7,000 miles out of it before it retired. It was getting me around town with no problem, so naturally I thought we could take it on our vacation to the mountains.

Did I mention the lodge is 600 miles away?

We could have taken Dale's Escape. Marcus drove up separately, so we had room for all our gear, the two of us, and the two dogs. But Dale doesn't like dog hair in his car. Besides, the van was in great shape.

Or so I thought.

A few miles down the freeway, the minivan began to jerk. "Jerk" is a mild term. It felt more like it was trying to buck us out of the car, but only occasionally. Since it was not constant and the car otherwise seemed happy, we kept going.

When Dale was behind the wheel, he tended to let it have its little tantrums. When I took over in Sacramento, I was determined to show the minivan who was in charge. Every time the car bucked, I stepped on the accelerator.

Did I mention the road from Sacramento to Truckee is almost entirely uphill?

At the top of the highest point, the van acknowledged me as its leader. It also began to flash the "Service Engine Soon" light in protest. This is when the praying began.

"Dear God, just get us back to our driveway next Sunday and I'll give up and buy a new car," I muttered under my breath.

Once we reached our destination, the service light went away and the van behaved like the angel it is. We spent five glorious days visiting lakes, hiking trails and having a great time. As we started down the mountain, I thought my car problems were over. I didn't need a new car after all.

When the bucking began again, I told God, "All right, I give up." As if to solidify my promise, as we pulled into the hotel in Sacramento, the driver's side window did not raise when I pressed the button. I wiggled the switch until it finally staggered to a mostly-closed position, with just a sliver of air still exposed.

This meant we drove all the way home on Sunday with the whoosh of road noise to drown out anything on the radio, or in our minds. We pulled into the driveway and I said four words I thought I'd never say.

"I hate this car."

I spent Sunday night researching, Monday morning test-driving, and on Thursday, drove home in a 2013 Ford Edge. My plan was to donate the minivan to a church, however, the dealership was having a trade-in rebate. I admit, I wept a little as I waved goodbye to the little white van in my rearview mirror.

In reality, I know how blessed I am and believe God takes care of me without any "deals." I guess I just like making Him laugh.

SPELLING RELIEF "S-A-F-E"

I think I mentioned last week that Marcus did not ride up with us to the mountains. He was in San Antonio with some friends for a convention when we left. They returned home on Sunday, he rested on Monday, then drove up on Tuesday.

It's a lot easier to explain now that I know he made it safely to his destination. At the time, it felt like the longest Tuesday of my life.

The lodge where we stay is in the Plumas National Forest, a little less than two hours northwest of Truckee. It's almost 600 miles from our house, and quite woodsy. As you can imagine, nighttime is dark and substantial. I warned Marcus of this, several times.

"Make sure you start early enough to get here before dark."

He nodded, in that way your kids nod when they hope it will make you stop talking. I gave him the address and phone number of the lodge, then I texted it to him, then I sent him an instant message. Then I asked him if he had the information.

No wonder he nods.

On Tuesday, I awoke wondering if my son had gotten on the road yet. Dale went golfing with some of the guys, and I went on a hike to a waterfall with the rest of our group. I tried really hard to not mention my son's name, or look at my watch.

My friends were kind enough to not point it out when I did.

We came back to the lodge and my friend Linda suggested I call Marcus from the lodge phone. There is no cell phone service in the forest, so I wouldn't have gotten any message he might have sent.

He answered his phone on the third ring.

"Where are you?" I asked.

"On the 5."

That did not surprise me. The I-5 to Sacramento is the standard route to take. "I figured that. How far up on the 5?"

"I don't know."

"Well, what town did you pass last?"

"I don't know."

I hung up, comforted at hearing his voice and wondering where the heck he was. We spoke one more time, a few hours later, when he told me he was near a town that sounded like he was too far north and would be coming in the long way. The sun was waning, but he was upbeat.

"I'm following my GPS," he chirped. "I should be there soon."

I tried not to think about all the silly people who have followed their GPS into lakes.

We all sat down to dinner as the last of the sunlight greyed to dusk. Suddenly I heard one of the girls say my favorite sentence of all time.

"Marcus is here."

Technically, it wasn't dark yet, so he managed to follow my suggestion, even if it was by the skin of his teeth and probably shaved a year off my life.

Once he was safe, I thought about myself around that age. When I was 24, I drove from Illinois to Fullerton in my Honda Civic, my little dog riding shotgun. We had no cell phones or GPS, although I did have a map. I'm pretty certain I didn't even call from the road every night.

Just like my son, I knew where I was going, and I knew I was alright.

WHEN LIFE HAS OTHER PLANS

For as busy as I am, I don't travel a lot. We take one weeklong vacation every year, and there are a couple of weekend trips to conferences, but most of the time I am scurrying around local places.

I've only been to Europe once, when Dale and I visited Paris and Italy. I keep thinking it was about four years ago, but Marcus was in 4th grade at the time. That's more like a dozen years.

This meant our recent trip to Scotland was a really big deal. I made lists of the things I had to do, and then broke those lists down into more detailed lists. I bought new shoes and extra socks. I cleaned the house so vigorously, I broke the vacuum.

Seriously, who cracks the canister on a Dyson?

The weekend before we left, I still had things to do. On Friday, I was due to get my temporary crown replaced with a permanent one. The dogs needed a bath and my bedroom needed cleaning. I was on track, though, to be on that plane Monday morning.

And then, life intervened.

I went to bed Thursday night feeling a little uncomfortable, thinking it was heartburn. By one o'clock in the morning, my chest felt like it was being squeezed by King Kong. I decided not to be stupid and woke Dale.

"Can you take me to the emergency room? I may be having a heart attack."

I always imagine ERs to be like the ones on TV, full of activity and ambulances and patients being wheeled in left and right. Placentia-Linda Hospital is not like that. There were two people in the waiting area, looking sleepy, and all the hospital personnel were behind a glass window.

The receptionist handed me a clipboard and told me to fill out my information.

"What can we help you with tonight?" she asked.

By now the pain was pretty severe. "My chest hurts," I squeaked.

That got their attention, and seconds later, I was lying in an alcove with wires hooked all over. Attendants fretted over me, sending me to x-rays and scans of all sorts. Eventually, a nice doctor came around, a clipboard in his hand and a smile on his face.

"Good news, your heart is fine," he said. "But your gallbladder is inflamed."

He discussed all my options, most of which involved surgery.

"Is this where I tell you I'm leaving for Scotland on Monday?" I asked. I might not have been so adamant about my trip if I was still in pain, but they'd started an IV with some kind of concoction that relaxed everything, including my gallbladder.

"Then surgery will wait," he said, still smiling.

They kept me a day for observation, but there was nothing much to observe, so I was sent home with pain pills and a promise that I'd eat small, low-fat meals and call my regular doctor upon my return.

My temporary crown didn't get replaced and the dogs never got their bath, but I still left for Scotland as scheduled. I tried to eat low-fat, but it was difficult to do in the land of fish and chips and sticky toffee pudding. In the end, I ate small amounts of whatever I wanted and set the pain pills on the nightstand just in case.

I never needed them, and Scotland was wonderful.

WISHING INDEPENDENCE FOR THE KIDS

Having a son in his last year of college is an exercise in patience. Maybe he'll go to graduate school. Maybe he won't. Maybe he'll find work in his field. Maybe not.

In the meantime, I'm still waiting to turn his bedroom into an office. He might return to the nest.

I was talking to a friend about the many grown children who either still live with their parents, or move back in when they fall on hard times. The friend, who is about my age, and I both agreed that when we were in our twenties, we did just about anything to move out of our parents' homes.

And we often ate crackers and peanut butter to keep from moving back.

I won't say that life was better 25 years ago. I will say it was different. When I moved out of my parents' house, my first apartment was furnished from garage sales. The only thing I bought new was from the local hardware store—I purchased cinder blocks and wood planks to serve as my shelving.

We're fortunate. Even though he has lived in various apartments for the last three years, Marcus has not expected us to provide for him in the style to which he is accustomed. Although, if we provided furniture like we have at home, it would have to be previously clawed by a cat and have residual dog hair.

For his first apartment, our son traveled around one day in my minivan with a copy of Craigslist by his side, and bought everything he needed for about $100. It was with great sadness I had to tell him, when he needs to move again, the new car doesn't have enough room for his table and chairs.

Preparing for life was also different when I was young. During high school, I had taken a lot of what they now call Advanced Placement classes. My school decided that all of the students preparing for college were not adequately taught about life, so we were all required to take a course called "Consumer Education." We learned about loans and interest, and even how to write a check.

I wish they'd bring that class back.

So far, Marcus has come to us to learn how to fill out a rental agreement and write checks. When he first went off to school with his brand new debit card, there was a month or two of learning curve, where he had to learn to track his expenses and make certain he wasn't overdrawn.

Fortunately, he was a quick study.

He was also wisely cynical about the pile of credit card offers he received every week. My opinion of credit card companies who prey on college students is not printable in a family newspaper. This is a slippery slope, one that Marcus could have launched himself down without our knowledge.

Instead, he laughed. "Why would I borrow money if I can't pay it back?"

It took me years to convince a company that I had a steady job and could be trusted with a credit card, and I had to convince myself that I could pay them back.

I guess, no matter what path our son chooses, we've done our best to raise him. Even if he comes home for a while, he can always sleep in the guest room. I could really use that office.

MARITAL ADVICE IS OFTEN SIMPLE

I love to read advice columns, even though the letters usually give me a feeling of "well, duh." When the problems involve marriage, however, I'm less sure of the advice.

How can one person solve their problem if it involves someone else?

Dale and I have been married for well over twenty years. We've survived the seven-year itch without a scratch, and we're currently adjusting to Dale's retirement.

If I had paid attention to advice columns, we may not have lasted this long.

Experts think you should have clear, constant communication with your spouse. This would not work with Dale and me. Dale's communication is a perfect example of the engineering mind: everything is on a "need to know" basis.

Despite my previous life as an engineer, I tend to over-share with my husband and prattle about daily trivia. I learned early in our marriage, until something becomes important enough to mention, Dale won't mention it.

Dale learned to nod at intervals while I babble.

Our recent evening at the Placentia Library illustrated this. We were there as guests of the library's Friends Foundation. Each year they have a Jewel Reception to honor patrons who have joined the Friends at the "jewel" level of membership.

It was a lovely event, as usual. We had good food, entertainment by a local high school, and brief speeches by the Friends President Zoot Velasco, Board of Trustees Secretary Elizabeth Minter, and Library Director Jeanette Contraras. I always enjoy this time to talk to old friends and meet new ones.

Dale has had plantar fasciitis since before Christmas. I didn't know about it until I mentioned his limping. Dale has injured himself in so many ways, I thought perhaps it was due to his bad knees or a residual of his torn Achilles.

He begrudgingly admitted his heel problems when I asked. I think his basic belief is, if I can't cure him, there's no use telling me.

At the reception, Trustee Richard Devecchio greeted us.

"You seem to be limping," he told Dale. "Did you injure yourself?"

"That's his normal walk," I said. I suppose I didn't really mean it was normal, but I've been watching him limp for quite a while.

Dale frowned at me. "This is not my normal walk."

He then explained his condition and he and Richard shared stories of foot injuries and what to do about them. Richard asked if he was considering surgery.

"No, I'm just going to play through the pain," Dale said.

This began a spirited discussion at our table about injuries and surgeries and what people were willing to trade for their health. Everyone was retired, which meant we are all at an age where we fight time and gravity for control of our bodies.

The man sitting next to me needed surgery on his foot, but knew a three month recuperation would interfere with his exercise routine, which would be bad for his blood pressure. His wife nodded in agreement, talking about how he avoided taking medication by changing his lifestyle.

I wouldn't know if Dale changed his lifestyle unless he turned the family room into a gymnasium. We're obviously not like the couple at the table, but our relationship works.

If I had to give marriage advice, I'd probably say ignore the experts and do what works for you and your spouse. That's my version of "well, duh" advice.

MAKING HAPPY CHOICES

Moms have a common language, with phrases that are universal. What mother hasn't warned her child not to do something because they'll put their eye out, or break their neck?

The other day, my horse trainer Niki was telling me about her 3-year-old. There had been a disruptive child at his daycare, and Tyler had been affected by his behavior. Once the child was no longer in his class, Tyler was back to his old self.

"Last week I made sad choices," he told his mom. "But this week I'm making happy choices."

It was obvious Niki had been using one of the classic Mom Phrases: "Make good choices."

I've told Marcus this for most of his childhood, more so during his teen years, and I may have said it every other sentence on his 21st birthday. So far, he's been listening. He hasn't put out an eye, or broken his neck. As to good choices, I guess what I don't know won't hurt me.

What I do know is often bad enough.

Recently, Marcus was chatting with me over the internet. It was late, and he'd been driving from one ATM to another, looking for one that would take his deposit. It seems all our credit union's ATMs were down, probably for maintenance.

I gave him my best mom advice. A long time ago, a credit union representative told me that we could make deposits at other banks' ATMs, but there'd be a hold of up to a week on the funds.

"That won't do," Marcus said when I explained it to him.

"Maybe the ATM outside our branch is working. If not, I guess you have to wait until the credit union opens tomorrow."

I went to bed and didn't think any more about it. Midway through the following day, I sent him a message, asking if he got his banking done.

"Finally," he responded. "The machine at our branch wasn't working, either. By that time, I was out of gas, so I slept in my car until the credit union opened."

Hear that sound? That's a mom's heart breaking.

I realize it was just a few hours. It was unlikely he was ever in any danger. He's not homeless, I could have reached him by phone. It was not a big deal. Still…

Why didn't he ask me for a few dollars to get him through to the next day? I could have transferred money to his account. I could have met him at a gas station. Or would that enable him, to always count on me to bail him out?

None of these choices seem like happy ones.

It is a parent's constant conundrum. Help your kids too much and they will never learn how to be independent. Help them too little and they're sleeping in their car in the credit union parking lot.

Either way, you're left with the weight of parental guilt.

Today, I asked Niki how Tyler's choices were going. "Oh, he's doing great in daycare, but I think dealing with a 3-year-old is worse than the terrible twos."

Tyler has learned a phrase of his own. When he is unhappy about anything, he tells his mom, "I'm not okay with this."

I can't approve of children saying that, but it might be a good one to add to the Mom Phrase list. I'm pretty sure there are many things we're not okay with.

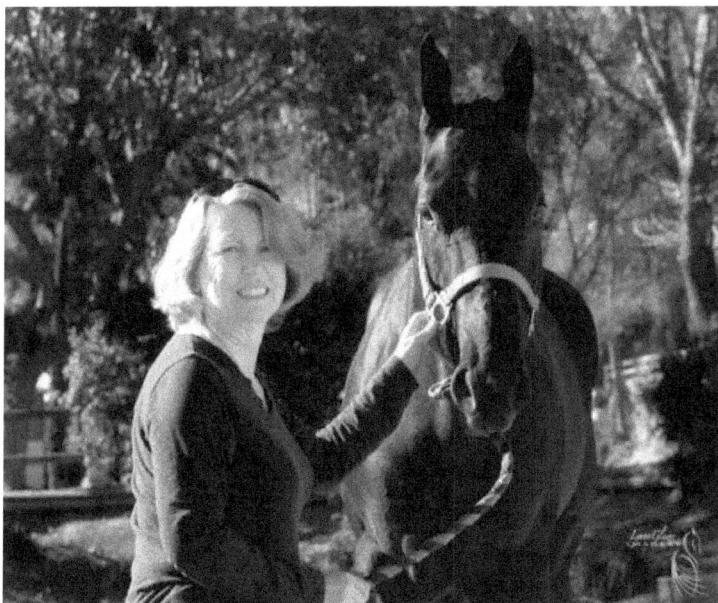

ABOUT THE AUTHOR

Gayle Carline is a typical Californian, meaning she was born somewhere else. She moved to Orange County from Illinois in 1978, and landed in Placentia a few years later.

Her husband, Dale, bought her a laptop for Christmas in 1999 because she wanted to write. A year after that, he gave her horseback riding lessons. When she bought her first horse, she finally started writing.

Gayle soon became a regular contributor to California Riding Magazine, and in March, 2005, she began writing a humor column for her local newspaper, the Placentia News-Times. Every week, she entertains readers with stories of her life with Dale and their son, Marcus.

Believing she should experience reincarnation while she is still alive, Gayle has been a software engineer, a dancer, and even a flying angel for the Crystal Cathedral's Glory of Christmas.

In her spare time, Gayle likes to sit down with friends and laugh over a glass of wine. Or two.

For more merriment, visit her at **http://www.gaylecarline.com**.

ALSO BY THIS AUTHOR

Freezer Burn (A Peri Minneopa Mystery)
Hit or Missus (A Peri Minneopa Mystery)
The Hot Mess (A Peri Minneopa Mystery)
Clean Sweep (A Peri Minneopa Short Story)

Murder on the Hoof

From the Horse's Mouth: One Lucky Memoir

What Would Erma Do? Confessions of a First Time
Humor Columnist
Are You There, Erma? It's Me Gayle
You're from Where?
Holly Jolly Holidays

www.ingramcontent.com/pod-product-compliance
Lightning Source LLC
LaVergne TN
LVHW051402080426
835508LV00022B/2941